1975

may be kept

FOURTEE   S

FolkSongs
& Singing
Games

David S. McIntosh

EDITED BY DALE WHITESIDE   ILLUSTRATIONS BY GREG TRAFIDLO

Southern Illinois University Press   CARBONDALE & EDWARDSVILLE

Feffer & Simons, Inc.   LONDON & AMSTERDAM

of the Illinois Ozarks

Library of Congress Cataloging in Publication Data

McIntosh, David Seneff, 1897–   comp.
    Folk songs and singing games of the Illinois Ozarks.

    Bibliography: p.
    1.   Folk-songs, American—Illinois.   2.   Singing games,
American.   I.   Title.
M1629.M1515F6   784.4′9773   72–75329
ISBN 0–8093–0585–2

The descriptions of "Molly Brooks" and "Goin' Down to Cairo"
are based on similar descriptions in *Singing Games and Dances*
by David S. McIntosh, copyright © 1957 by Association Press,
291 Broadway, New York, New York 10007.

CONTENTS

INTRODUCTION

Professor David McIntosh has presented to students of folklore and to the residents of the Illinois Ozarks a gift which no amounts of technology or capital can produce. For more than thirty-five years he pursued folk music in the "thirty-two counties," a project which grew out of his love of this part of the country and of Southern Illinoisans who, in my experience, identify with their surroundings more than most Americans. To support this position I point out only one of many obvious facts: people from Rock Island, Sterling, Elgin, or Wheaton say, "I'm from Illinois"; people from Metropolis, West Frankfort, Jonesboro, or Mt. Vernon say, "I'm from Southern Illinois." Outsiders, even other Illinoisans, are generally unaware of this feeling of community which exists in the "thirty-two counties." Such feelings of identity greatly reduce the thankless quality of much of the folklorist's work.

Folklore seems to occupy a curious position in the social psychology of literate peoples. While each of us possesses a store of knowledge which could be labeled "lore," few among us consider it much of an asset. The information is perhaps of too recent origin to qualify as gems of wisdom or insights into humanity. Yet it is this very kind of understanding for which historians, anthropologists, social scientists of every bent are rewarded and praised. The aspects of contemporary life with which we are quite familiar through personal experience or through accounts heard from our elders are normally relegated to insignificance, often blinding us to the marvels which might be occurring in our own backyard. The fence which separates us from "greener grass" may be of two types: place, which makes Tahiti or New Zealand sources of fascination; or time, which might bring us to relish an old book entitled, *Scientific Sidelights*, whereas we perhaps never open a recent volume pertaining to science of any kind. Given this attitude among his fellows, the folklorist looks farther than most students for material support in his work.

Professor McIntosh's first collection tour was made with a specific purpose in mind—the compilation of his master's thesis at the University of Iowa. Although the thesis is a massive document, it constitutes only a small portion of the total collection, for, upon moving to Carbondale, he and his wife, Eva, continued the work. In the thirties the folklorist had little or no equipment such as recording machines. The McIntoshes did their early work armed only with pencils, music manuscript paper, and good ears. Transcribing alternate lines, the team collected in this fashion until the Soundscriber became available. This magic box enabled them both to cut records and to play them back to determine the quality of the recording. Some years later, of course, the tape recorder replaced the Soundscriber.

Traveling to communities throughout the Illinois Ozarks, they amassed a broad sample of music which was used by the people here. Folk music, in one definition, is closely connected with an oral tradition. A folk song or children's singing game or rope-jumping rhyme is a piece of culture passed along from parent to child or from child to child, etc. This body of orally transmitted knowledge dwindles as society becomes increasingly print-oriented, and as the children spend less time with their families in favor of school classrooms, playgrounds, summer day-camps, and lessons in music or dance.

As this kind of social change advances, the young learn more and more from books, school music instructors, and recreation leaders. Thus the folk traditions, in the purest sense of the word, are waning under the onslaught of the mass media. Many folklorists are motivated by one or both of two emotions. The first is a conservative drive which decries any change resulting in the loss of his pet folk traditions. The second is perhaps a more realistic and objective stance—that change *is* part of life and part of social existence, but that records should be made of each time stratum. In this way, information and content are available for present and future study. Such is the essence of folklore and folklorists.

As folklorists, David and Eva McIntosh have, I am certain, felt both of these thrusts. Which of us who claims an interest in his fellowman fails to feel pain at the loss of a tradition like family singing? And which student or scholar of history does not regret deeply the unfortunate efficiency with which the Spanish conquistadores concealed and destroyed all but a few vestiges of New World indigenous culture?

The McIntosh passion surpassed the limits of a purely scholarly process. Both learned to sing many of the songs they collected, and they performed them for all who wished to hear. The magnitude of their collection presents a staggering challenge which is met, in part, by the present volume. Before the story made possible by the McIntosh perseverance is told, many such volumes will have to appear.

The present volume represents a selection of traditional material which the author felt to be of special interest to the people of the Illinois Ozarks of today. It can be a pleasurable experience for the casual reader, enlightening for the folklorist, and a source of new material for the performer of folk music.

The people of the Illinois Ozarks can be truly proud of David McIntosh, who has labored quietly and diligently to preserve a part of their heritage, and who has found it a source of pride to number himself among them.

DALE WHITESIDE

Southern Illinois University
August 1973

ACKNOWLEDGMENTS

In the preparation of this collection of oral lore we are indebted to the author-collector and his wife, Professor and Mrs. David S. McIntosh, who live in retirement in Makanda, and who have lent their entire collection to the Project in Ethnomusicology, University Museum, for research purposes. I also would like to acknowledge with much gratefulness the countless hours of assistance in the form of advice from Dr. Carroll L. Riley and Dr. B. C. Hedrick; typing and proofreading by Mrs. Virginia Karnes, administrative secretary; and Kathy Abbass, Jon Steele, Susan Vinson, and Maureen O'Neill, student assistants. For additional advice we thank Dr. Alan Oldfield of the School of Music, Dr. and Mrs. John Gardner, and Mrs. Brent Riley. Finally, I thank my own invaluable assistants, Gregg Fisher, John Duner, Ken Krauss, and Katherine Peters, and particularly Phyllis DePriest, who share my enthusiasm for the work done by David McIntosh and for the people who inspired him to do it.

D. W.

Part 1

Local Songs and Ballads

INTRODUCTION

For convenience, we have divided this part into two chapters in order to differentiate between the traditional songs and ballads that came into the Illinois Ozarks as part of the folk heritage of the early settlers, and those songs and ballads that either originated here or have become attached to some particular locality in this region. The imported folk songs are variant versions of widely distributed texts. Locally, they have been perpetuated purely out of the love of singing, without any special significance being attached to them. The same thing can be said about two or three of the local songs, which appear to be adaptations to the local environment. Most of those included, however, arose strictly out of local situations. An effort has been made to include a variety of themes; but, the most significant items, no doubt, are those based on the themes of violence and disaster, which are common themes also among the traditional ballads of English and Scottish origin. We have omitted two ballads dealing with the violent deaths of two local bad men—Charlie Birger and Carl Shelton. Neely, in *Tales and Songs of Southern Illinois*,[1] has published a version of "The Death of Charlie Birger." The author is unknown. The Shelton ballad is said to have been composed by Earl Shelton, the brother of Carl. Both ballads have been recorded, but copies are something of a rarity today.

"La Gui-Annee," which poses interesting problems and mysteries to the folklorist, is "localized" rather than "local," having originated elsewhere but today surviving in only one small pocket of this area.

Songs of Local Significance

"LA GUI-ANNEE"

One of the earliest traditional songs brought in by the French, and still sung on New Year's Eve in Prairie du Rocher, Illinois, and Saint Genevieve, Missouri, is "La Gui-Annee." In the bicentennial edition of the *Saint Genevieve Herald*,[2] August 17, 1935, the words of the song are given in French, German, and English, with the following introduction:

> The name of this quaint old song has puzzled many as to its derivation, and that even its orthography has become perverted is evidenced by the fact that it is spelled "La Guiannee," "La Gaie-Anne," and "La Guignolee," each according to individual interpretation. Some claim it comes from a custom among the ancient Druid priests in the north of France. Others hold that it is a Creole song, no more or less, probably of Canadian origin, as they claim is proved by the style and language, and the dance is interpreted as purely an imitation of an Indian dance. . . . The old custom handed down from early settlers is religiously adhered to in Saint Genevieve, and in later years local womenfolk have taken up the custom of "running 'La Gui-Annee' " independent of the men.

The traditional character of this song is indicated by the variations in the French lyrics and in the tune. "La Gui-Annee," by Anne Andre Clark, was published as a souvenir of the rededication of the Cahokia courthouse, Cahokia, Illinois, on May 29–30, 1940. French and English lyrics are printed on the back and the music is arranged for piano. The title page gives this additional information:

> Before midnight the townspeople have joined this band and all gather in the Town Hall, where the ball is opened by the masqueraders

selecting a partner from the ladies in the audience, which is a great honor, and the dancing and feasting is carried on until the bells ring for the early mass celebration on New Year's Day.

This publication by Miss Clark of "La Gui-Annee," is identical to one copyrighted in 1914 by Mrs. Charles P. Johnson, harmonized by Ernest R. Kroeger, and published by Kunkel Brothers Music Company.

Mr. John Allen, formerly of the Southern Illinois University staff, and I recorded this song in the barber shop in Prairie du Rocher at nine o'clock, New Year's Eve, December 31, 1943, before the singers started on their visits to the homes. Later we were in the home of Mr. Tom Conner when the singers came. The first part of the song was sung on the front porch. The host invited the group of fifteen singers and one fiddle player in, and, without stopping their singing, they trouped into the living room and finished their song. Drinks and cakes or cookies, made for the occasion, were served to all. The group then went on to another house.

Just before midnight, in the local combination bar and ice-cream parlor, we were surprised to see that all the singers were still able to navigate. They had come to wish everyone well and to drink a toast to the New Year.

The song is sung antiphonally, with one or two leaders singing a phrase which is then repeated by the group. Throughout the entire song, the phrases are four measures in length, with the exception of the epilogue, or leader's solo, which varies according to the vocal condition of the leader and the inspiration of the moment. The last two phrases are sung by the entire group, while the fiddler plays the melody throughout the entire song.

SOURCE: *Anne Andre Clark, Cahokia, Illinois, May 29–30, 1940.*

Good mas-ter and mis-tress of this house and the lod-gers
Bon--soir le maî-tre et la maî-tresse, et tout le

all, good night to you, for the last day of the end-
mon- de du lo-gis, pour le der-nier jour de l'

ing year, the Gui - an-nee is to us due. If it is
an - née, la guig - no-lee vous nous de - vez. Si vous

no-thing you will give them let us know we on-ly
ne vou - lez nous rien don -ner dites-nous le, nous vous

ask a pork-back-bone you should be-stow. A pork-
de-man-dons seu-le-ment une é - chi-née. Une é -

back-bone is no great prize 'tis on - ly four
chi - née n'est pas grand-chose elle n'a que qua-tre

feet long in size, with it we make fri-ca-ssée
pieds de long, et nous en fer-ons une fri-ca-ssée

that ten , and eight feet in length shall be. If you will
de quatr-vingt-dix pieds de long. Si vous

no-thing give us more please let us hear we on-ly
ne vou- lez nous rien don - ner dites-nous le, nous vous

ask the el- dest daugh- ter to ap-pear.   With
de- man-dons seu- le-ment la fil-le ain--née. Et

jol - ly good cheer we   will her greet and we will
nous lui fer- ons faire bon- ne chère, nous lui fer-

warm her chil-ly feet. When we   were in   the
ons chauf-fer les pieds. Quand nous   fûmes aux

midst of woods in   sha - ded grove,   we lis- ten
milieux des bois nous fûmes a l'om - bre, j'ai en -ten-

to the cuck-oo sing   and the tur-tle dove   and the
du le cou-cou chan-ter et le co - - lom-be et le

night-in-gale of the bow-er green, as her--ald   of
ro - sig-nol du   vert bo-cage, l'am bas-sa-deur des

love   will   go and say that   ev- er my heart is
a-mour-eux va al-ler dire qu'elle ait tou - jours le

joy-ous, gay. My   heart is ev - er filled with joy
coeur joy-eux. Qu'elle ait tou-jours le coeur joy- eux

and   sor-rows not,   but all the young   girls
point de   tris-tesse, mais ces   jeunes filles

who   are love - less, what is   their   lot? It is
qu'ont pas d'amants com - ment font el - les? Ce

love's ef-fect   that keeps them wake   and will not al-
sont   les amours qui les   re - veillent et   qui les

low ^ them rest to   take and now for your kind-ness
em-pê-chent de   dor- mir bon soir le   maî- tre et

with de- light   we thank the house-hold and wish good-
la   maî-tresse et tout le mon - de   du lo -

night. We sup-pli-cate the com-pa -ny   to be will-
gis.   Nous sup-pli-ons la com-pag-nie d'- vou-loir

ing to   ex-cuse us   if we   have com - mit-ted a - ny
bien nous ex-cu - ser si nous a - vons fait   quel-que

fol-ly it was for our re-cre-a - tion and a-noth-er
fol-ie c'e-tait pour nous de-sen-nu- yer une   aut -re

time we   will take care if we   have the   hap-pi-
fois nous pren-drons garde si nous a - vons le bon -

ness   to re - turn.
heur de re- ven- nir.

"ALAN BANE"

The song "Alan Bane" came into existence because of a near-hanging at Benton, Illinois, in 1866. The following information came from Lena Moore, 407 East Church, Benton, Illinois, April 24, 1951: [3]

> One of the most remarkable cases that was ever tried in Franklin County was in the old courthouse, built in 1845, wherein an innocent man became in danger upon circumstantial evidence of having to suffer the penalty for the crime of murder. It was the case of the *People* v. *David Williams*. He was accused of killing a man named McMahan.

> In the early part of 1866, the remains of a human body were found about two miles southeast of Benton on top of a fallen tree, and were supposed to be the remains of Mr. McMahan. A coroner's inquest was held, and upon the verdict of the jury, Williams was arrested.

> Later he was tried before Judge A. D. Duff. He was prosecuted by T. J. Layman, Sr. and defended by F. M. Youngblood. The evidence was that the last seen of McMahan, he was in the company of Williams, and that he had several hundred dollars in his possession. A pocketknife found with the remains was identified as one belonging to McMahan. The hair of the victim was red, and so was McMahan's, and certain teeth of the dead man were removed, corresponding with the lost teeth of McMahan. The People, through their attorney, were making a strong case on circumstantial evidence.

> On the second day of the trial, when the evidence was nearly closed and the guilt of the prisoner fully established in the minds of those who had heard the evidence, the closing scene of the tragedy was enacted. Just at this critical moment, the supposed murdered man, McMahan, deliberately, and to the great astonishment of all, walked into the courtroom. He was immediately identified by a number of his former acquaintances and also by the witnesses on whose testimony the case was being made against the prisoner. This, of course, put an end to all further proceedings against the prisoner, and he was set free.

> Reuben Drummond, who knew of these parties, and knew of the prosecution of Mr. Williams, happened to be at the depot at DuQuoin and saw McMahan among the passengers on the Illinois Central train. He boarded the train and prevailed upon McMahan to get off the train at Tamaroa and come to Benton to save the man who was being prosecuted for his murder. Mr. McMahan rented a

horse from the livery stable in Tamaroa and rode to Benton, arriving at a very opportune time.

It is not publicly known who the murdered man was, but from certain incidents which came to light, he was supposed to have been a gambler who had been killed by another gambler in an old house on the south side of what is now West Main Street. The house, being unoccupied at the time, was a resort for gamblers. It was supposed that some strangers of that profession had congregated there and quarrelled, one of their number being killed and his body concealed in the fallen tree.

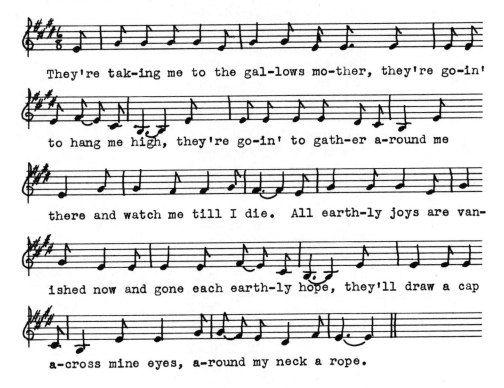

They're tak-ing me to the gal-lows mo-ther, they're go-in'
to hang me high, they're go-in' to gath-er a-round me
there and watch me till I die. All earth-ly joys are van-
ished now and gone each earth-ly hope, they'll draw a cap
a-cross mine eyes, a-round my neck a rope.

1. They're taking me to the gallows mother,
    They're goin' to hang me high,
    They're goin' to gather around me there
    And watch me till I die.
    All earthly joys are vanished now
    And gone each earthly hope;
    They'll draw a cap across mine eyes,
    Around my neck a rope.

2.   The crazy mob will shout and groan,
The priest will read a prayer,
The drop will fall beneath my feet
And leave me in the air.
They think I murdered Alan Bane,
For so the judge has said;
They'll hang me to the gallows, Ma.
And hang me 'til I'm dead.

3.   The grass that grows in yonder field,
The lambs that skip and play,
The brook that 'yond the orchard runs
And laughs upon the way.
The flowers that in the garden bloom,
The birds that sing and fly
Are pure and clean from human blood,
And Mother, so am I.

4.   My father's grave on yonder hill,
His name without a stain,
I swear no malice e'er I had
Nor murdered Alan Bane.
But me the jury guilty found,
For so the judge has said;
They'll hang me to the gallows, Ma,
And hang me 'til I'm dead.

5.   The air is fresh and bracing, Ma,
The sun shines bright and high,
This is a pleasant day to live,
A gloomy one to die.
This is a bright, a glorious day,
The joys of earth to grasp;
It is a sad, a wretched one
To struggle, choke, and gasp.

6.   Let them my lofty spirit damp,
Or cow me if they can,
They've sent me like a rogue to die,
I'll meet it like a man.
I never murdered Alan Bane,
But so the judge has said;
They'll hang me to the gallows, Ma,
And hang me 'til I'm dead.

7. Poor little sister Belle will weep
    And kiss me as I lie,
    But kiss her twice and thrice for me
    And tell her not to cry.
    Tell her to weave a garland gay
    And crown me as of yore
    And plant a lily on my grave
    And think of me no more.

8. And tell the maid whose love I sought,
    That I am faithful yet,
    But I'm to lie in a felon's grave
    And she had best forget.
    My memory is forever stained,
    For so the judge has said;
    They'll hang me to the gallows, Ma,
    And hang me 'til I'm dead.

9. Lay me not down by father's side,
    For once I mind, he said
    No child that stained his spotless name
    Could share his mortal bed.
    Old friends will look beyond his grave
    To my dishonored one
    And hide the virtues of the sire
    Behind the recreant son.

10. And I can fancy that if there,
    My fettered limbs should lay,
    His frowning skull and crumbling bones
    Would shriek, drive me away.
    I swear to God I'm innocent
    And never blood have shed;
    They'll hang me to the gallows, Ma,
    And hang me 'til I'm dead.

11. You'll lay me in my coffin, Ma,
    As you have seen me rest,
    One of my arms beneath my head,
    The other on my breast.
    And place my Bible on my heart,
    Nay, Mother, do not weep
    But kiss me as in happier days
    You kissed me when asleep.

12. As for the rest, for rite or form
     But little do I lack,
     But cover up that cursed stain,
     The black mark on my neck,
     And pray to God for mercy great
     On my devoted head.
     They'll hang me to the gallows, Ma,
     And hang me 'til I'm dead.

13. But hark! I hear a murmur now
     Among the jostling crowd,
     A cry! A shout! A roar! It grows
     And echoes long and loud.
     Comes dashing on a foaming steed,
     A man with tightened rein,
     He sits erect, he waves his hand,
     Good God! It's Alan Bane!

14. The lost is found, the dead's alive,
     My safety is achieved.
     He waves his hand again and shouts:
     "The prisoner is reprieved!"
     Now Mother praise the God you love
     And raise your drooping head,
     The murd'rous gallows, black and grim
     Is cheated of its dead.

SOURCE: *Mr. Andrew Jackson Reynolds, Rudiment, Illinois, July 7, 1935.*

"FLOOD OF SHAWNEETOWN"

Both words and music to the song, "Flood of Shawneetown," or "Broken Hearts and Homes," were written by Mr. G. B. Fields and published by the author at Fairfield, Illinois, in 1898.

On Thursday, August 13, 1896, the *Shawnee News*,[4] of Shawneetown, Illinois, carried a lengthy account of the floods at Shawneetown as far back as 1832 with the history of the construction of the levees, the first of which was built in 1859. The levee, which is called the "faithful levee" in the song, built in 1884, was four miles in length, ten feet wide on top, and three feet higher than the flood of 1884, which rose to a height of sixty-six feet above the low-water mark.

The *Shawnee News*, April 14, 1898,[5] carried the following information: "It was Sunday afternoon, April 3, 1898, at five o'clock that the north levee gave way at Locust Street." This song is represented in my collection by four versions. In this version the chromatic tones found in the published copy have been deleted, and each verse is sung to the same tune.

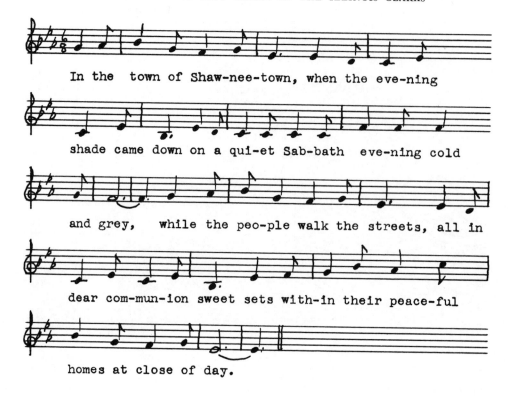

In the town of Shaw-nee-town, when the eve-ning

shade came down on a qui-et Sab-bath eve-ning cold

and grey, while the peo-ple walk the streets, all in

dear com-mun-ion sweet sets with-in their peace-ful

homes at close of day.

SOURCE: *Mr. Logan Bishop, Raleigh, Illinois.*

"THE WRECK AT MAUD"

This song will recall to mind another, better-known song about a railroad wreck in the Middle West, "Casey Jones." In an article in the *Tennessee Folklore Bulletin*,[6] Mr. Robert Y. Drake presents an excellent analysis of "Casey Jones." All of the statements that he makes about "Casey's" heroic character could be made about Al Bowen, the engineer hero of the "Maud Wreck." The similarity between the two songs is remarkable. Both trains were running late, both firemen jumped, both engineers, worthy and upright men, were killed. Interestingly, the two wrecks occurred about five years apart, "Casey's" wreck April 30, 1900, and the "Maud Wreck" on December 24, 1905.

On April 1, 1954, Miss Daisy May Stutsman, a student at Southern Illinois University, lent me a notebook of songs that she had learned from

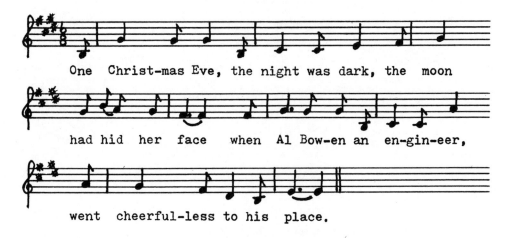

One Christ-mas Eve, the night was dark, the moon

had hid her face when Al Bow-en an en-gin-eer,

went cheerful-less to his place.

her mother who lives at St. Francisville, Illinois. The notebook contains a version with additional verses of the "Maud Wreck" with a note following concerning the wreck:

> Al had a smile, kind word for all
> A courteous man was he,
> His winning ways made many friends
> As many will agree.

> Before Al made that fatal trip
> He cheerfully did proclaim,
> "Good-bye, mother, if I never come back
> I'll always be the same."

> "Give her more coal," he said to Hulty
> "We must make up the time."
> To his surprise he saw a light
> Come streaming down the line.

NOTE: This happened between Maud and Mt. Carmel, Illinois, on the Southern Railroad (closer to Maud). This occurred when my father was a small boy, around 1905. Al Bowen, Hutchinson (Hulty), and McNeely were born and raised in Indiana. They made the run on the Southern early in the morning from Princeton, Indiana, to St. Louis, Missouri (Passenger trains—both).

Another version of this song obtained by Chlorene E. Blades from her mother, Mrs. Iva Wilson of Fairfield, Illinois, August 8, 1954, contains these additional verses:

> The Southern had no braver man
> No better engineer
> But Al that night
> He seemed to have a little lingering fear.
>
> There is no use to wish to stay
> No extra man have we
> I'll do my duty come what may
> What is to be will be.

The "Wreck at Maud" was recorded by Mr. Dies Burton at Flora, Illinois, where he made the following statement about the song:

> I can remember very little about this wreck; it probably was between fifty or sixty years ago, on account of the man that was the fireman on this train was a distant relative of my father's and I know from that, that it must have been about that time and this song is a true story of this wreck. It really happened. Maud is about six or eight miles west of Mt. Carmel. It's on the Southern Railroad, just a little wide place in the road.

SOURCE: *Mr. Dies Burton, Cisne, Illinois, May 1, 1952.*

"ACROSS THE PLAINS OF ILLINOIS"

"Across the Plains of Illinois" laments a situation almost universal in the folk traditions of England, Scotland, and America—the infidelity of a young woman while her suitor is away trying to make his mark in the world. While the setting is strictly "Illinoisan," the lyric echoes many earlier songs such as the English ballad, "So Early in the Morn."

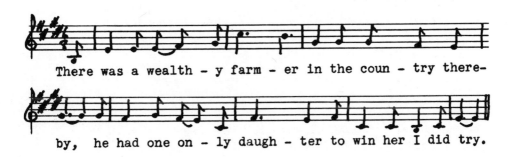

There was a wealth - y farm - er in the coun - try there-

by, he had one on - ly daugh - ter to win her I did try.

There was a wealthy farmer in the country thereby,
He had one only daughter, to win her I did try.

I asked her if it made any difference if I should
cross the plain,
If she'd ever prove untrue until I returned again.

She said it didn't make any difference if I should
cross the plain,
She would never prove untrue until I returned again.

I left old Illinois for Missouri I was bound,
I stepped off at Cairo to view the city around.

The work there it was plentiful and the girls to me
were kind,
But the only object of my heart was the girl I'd
left behind.

I got up early one morning, went out on public square,
The mailboat it was arriving and the newsboy he was there.

He handed to me a letter which give me to understand
The girl I'd left behind me, had married another man.

I turned around and around and around, I didn't know
what to do,
I went on over to Sikeston and found it all to be true.

Come all of you young gentlemen an' listen to my song,
I'm sure that if it does you no good, I'm sure it will
do you no harm.

If ever you're courting a pretty little miss, just
marry her while you can,
If you ever cross the plains, she'll marry another man.

SOURCE: *Mrs. Ollie Barnard, Cave-in-Rock, Illinois, May 2, 1954, by her
daughter Millie Barnard Angleton.*

CAMPAIGN SONGS

A little political history should clear up the issues represented in these campaign songs.

The campaign songs included in this volume revolve mainly around the presidential election of 1896 between William McKinley and William Jennings Bryan. The depression of the 1890s was felt hardest in the agrarian centers of the country, and the primary issue of the election was the monetary plank of the Democratic party which advocated the free coinage of silver at a ratio of 16 to 1 over the standard gold-based system. William Jennings Bryan championed the "free silver" cause in an impassioned speech before the Democratic Convention of 1896 and, as a result, won the party's nomination for president. Although William McKinley was not against "bimetallism," he feared an international monetary crises if the United States should adopt such a standard without first gaining the support of the other gold-based nations. As a result, the issue polarized the two parties and the country, and McKinley easily defeated the "silver Democrat," Bryan. The political affiliation of the songs is obvious.

Mr. R. H. Finley, who used to live in the area south of Carterville which is now covered by Crab Orchard Lake, described the parade mentioned in the third verse of "Way Over in Williamson." He said there were sixteen white horses and one yellow horse with sixteen girls dressed in white on the white horses, and one girl dressed in yellow on the yellow horse. These teams of horses were hitched to large wagons which had seats along the sides facing the center. These were called "band wagons," and the term "gettin' on the bandwagon" meant getting into one of these parade wagons. This particular parade started at Creal Springs, Illinois, and ended at Harrisburg, Illinois.

The "free silver" issue can be seen represented in the sixteen white horses (silver) and the one yellow horse (gold) with their respective riders.

"Way Over in Williamson"

This song was collected on May 19, 1934.

1. Don't you know Billy Bryan will never git there
   Don't you know? Don't you know?
   Billy McKinley will fill the chair.
   Don't you know? Don't you know?

Chorus:
>   Way over in Williamson
>   Away over in the county where we grow
>   Way over in Williamson
>   Don't you know? Don't you know?

2.   Don't you know Henry Jones will be our next clerk
>   Don't you know? Don't you know?
>   For H. P. Crain is big enough to work.
>   Don't you know? Don't you know?

3.   Sixteen to one makes the gold bug shiver
>   Don't you know? Don't you know?
>   Sixteen to one makes the gold bug shiver.
>   Don't you know? Don't you know?

SOURCE: *Mr. R. H. Finley, Carterville, Illinois, May 19, 1934.*

"Bye, Old Grover"

Verna Mae Wood, Collinsville, gave this account of "Old Grover" on November 29, 1949: "The song, 'Bye, Old Grover' was sung on the platform at a Republican rally in Alhambra, Illinois, in the year 1889 on the porch of the Reudy store, by a black quartet. Whole families for miles around attended this rally. My father took his family in a two horse wagon."

>   William Jennings Bryan
>   Sitting on the fence
>   Trying to make a dollar
>   Out of fifty cents.

> *Chorus*:
>   Bye, old Grover, bye, oh,
>   Bye, old Grover, bye.

>   I saw the train go 'round the curve,
>   Good-bye, old Grover, good-bye
>   All loaded down with Harrison's men
>   Good-bye, old Grover, good-bye.

SOURCE: *Verna Mae Wood, Collinsville, Illinois, November 8, 1949.*

"Wait for the Wagon"

Here is a version of a familiar old song that was used in the Illinois Ozarks with political content:

1. Wait for the wagon, the Free Silver Wagon,
   Wait for the wagon and we'll all take a ride.
2. Here comes the wagon, the Free Silver Wagon,
   Here comes the wagon and we'll all take a ride.
3. Hop on the wagon, the Free Silver Wagon,
   Hop on the wagon and we'll all take a ride.

SOURCE: *Mary K. Harris, Fairfield, Illinois, March 30, 1949.*

"There'll Be a Hot Time in the Old Town Tonight"

Another well-known tune, with a political slant to the words:

[*Tune*: "There'll Be a Hot Time in the Old Town Tonight"]
Me oh my just hear the people yell
If McKinley is elected our country's gone to—well
If we elect Billy Bryan, we'll all be living well.
There'll be a hot time in the old town tonight my honey.

SOURCE: *Faye Gilby, Salem, Illinois, January 16, 1952.*

COUNTY SONGS

Folk music, for some inexplicable reason, always seems more "traditional" when it treats situations or locations removed from us by distance, either temporal or geographic. The Illinois Ozarks, however, has its share of fine local songs touting its counties, jails, Illinois gals, and turnip greens. The "thirty-two counties" are also represented by songs treating the traditional themes of the hardships of pioneer life and the appreciation of the beauties of the area.

One of the songs included in this volume, "Jackson County," illustrates an aspect of the English broadside tradition, whereby one tune served for many sets of lyrics. "Jackson County" is sung to the tune of "Columbia, the Gem of the Ocean"; however, the author is unknown.

"Jackson County"

Oh Jackson, our County, we greet thee,
And sing with sweet Freedom's refrain,
While the echoes o'er valley and hillside
Resound with our country's high fame.
Oh, God of our country and nation,
Grant blessings of peace and good will
For the children of our dear old Jackson
And united we'll trust in thee still.

Chorus:
Three cheers for the County of Jackson!
Three cheers for the school houses, too!
Oh, Jackson the County forever,
Three cheers for old Jackson so true.

By the West flows the Father of Waters,
Rolling on past our Egypt's broad fields,
With the hills of Kinkaid for a landscape
Whose soil brings us forth her fair yields.
But the blessing most lovingly counted,
Are the children and youth of our land,
And when listed will number ten thousand
Happy-hearted bright juvenile band.

Oh, hero of old, General Jackson,
We sing thy brave deeds and thy fame,
Thy wisdom and power we honor
And always will cherish thy name.
May our rulers make anarchists tremble,
As the proud Ship of State sails along,
While the flag waves aloft its blue emblem,
Oh, Jackson, fair Jackson, our song.

In our pride for this County of Jackson,
May we give our best efforts in song,
With full hearts from its joys never sever,
Thus in union and service grow strong.
So determined and eager to follow
The example our father made plain,
With purpose and loyalty ever,
We join in this chorus again.

SOURCE: *Mrs. Mabel McGowan, Carbondale, Illinois, July 5, 1934.*

"Jackson County Jail"

Songs about jails, as seen from the inside, are common in traditional folklore. Whether the tenants are falsely or rightly accused, the songs usually end with a warning to the listener on how not to follow in the speaker's footsteps—in this case a plea to stop drinking and gambling. The tune that I used in singing the song, since my source had not been able to give me one, was "Come All Texas Rangers." Dating back to October 1931, I learned this tune from Mr. William Jones, who lived about seven miles south of Carbondale, Illinois.

After singing the following song for the business men's club in the county seat of Jackson County some years ago, I was informed by one

of the members that we had one of the finest jails in the country. I forgot
to ask him how he knew.

Come all ye roving gamblers,
And won't you be aware?
It's how you go to see them girls
A-standing on the square.
In Murphysboro city,
Be careful how you sail,
Or you'll find yourself all locked up
In the Jackson County jail.

I had an only partner,
Jim Lincoln was his name,
And when he got in trouble,
'Twas me he always blamed.
The first thing was to quarrel,
To fight he'd never fail,
And now he's got me locked up
In the Jackson County jail.

They took me before the honorable judge,
A dishonest judge was he,
They tried me for murder,
My disposition was.
They tried me for murder,
No one would go my bail,
And now they've got me locked up
In the Jackson County jail.

They took me to the jailhouse,
My room was number four,
They fed me on "corn dodger,"
But I often wanted more.
Their beds were of the finest,
To sleep I often failed,
You may bet the feathers were hard, boys,
In the Jackson County jail.

Last night as I lay sleeping,
I had a pleasant dream,
I dreamed I was down on "Muddy,"

Down by that crooked stream,
With my sweetheart beside me,
All ready to go my bail,
But I woke up broken hearted
In the Jackson County jail.

So now my song is ended,
A few words to you I'll say,
You'd better stop your drinking,
And throwing your money away.
You'd better stop your gambling,
And throwing your money about,
For when you get in the old jailhouse
You bet it's hard to get out.

SOURCE: *Mamie Hertz, Anna, Illinois, RR 2, October 20, 1947.*

"Illinois Gals"

Cecil J. Sharp in his *English Folk Songs from the Southern Appalachians* [7] gives one version similar to this.

This song, "Illinois Gals," gives advice to young women concerning matrimony and its consequences.

1. Come on Illinois gals and listen to my noise,
   You ought not to marry the swappin' boys,
   If you do your portion will be,
   Corn bread and black beans is all you'll see;
   Corn bread and black beans is all you'll see.

2. Drive you out on the post to kill,
   There they'll leave you much against your will,
   They'll leave you without a purse on the place,
   That's the way with the swappin' race;
   That's the way with the swappin' race.

3. When they get their milk, they get it in a gourd,
   Strain it in a wagon, covered with a board,
   Some get little, some get more.
   That's the way the swappin's run;
   That's the way the swappin's run.

4. When they go to meetin', what do you think they wear?
   Old blue coat, all pitched in hair,
   Old straw hat, all trimmed in crown,
   Old cotton socks that they wear the winter round;
   Old cotton socks that they wear the winter round.

SOURCE: *Lula Groves, Carmi, Illinois, from her uncle, Mr. Lot Bradford, Marshall, Illinois, February 9, 1950.*

"Turnip Greens"

A diet of corn bread, buttermilk, and turnip greens was the source of beauty for the girls of Salem, Illinois, if you can believe the creator of the song, "Turnip Greens."

The informant tells us that, "this song was sung by early settlers from the Ohio River valley who settled in and near Salem, Illinois."

1. I had a dream the other night,
    I dreamed that I could fly,
    I flapped my wings like a buzzard,
    And flew up to the sky.

Chorus:
    Turnip greens, turnip greens,
    Corn bread and buttermilk,
    And a dish of turnip greens.

2. At the gate I met St. Peter,
    He stood upon his feet,
    He asked me in to dinner,
    And this is what we eat.

3. He asked me where I came from,
    At which I prompt replied,
    I just came in from Salem,
    And this is what we pride.

4. Oh, these pretty girls of Salem,
    They always look so neat,
    All from corn bread and buttermilk,
    And good old turnip greens.

SOURCE: *Grandpa Decker, McLeansboro, Illinois, March 17, 1953.*

"Sweet Marie"

The song "Sweet Marie," is concerned with one of the hardships of the pioneers. Only one who has experienced an attack of malaria can appreciate the faith of the young man in the song.

1. A few more skeeter bites, sweet Marie,
    A few more quinine pills, sweet Marie,
    Will make a wreck of me, sweet Marie.
    I'll get rid of ague, yet
    I've got the framework yet,
    We'll be happy yet, you bet, sweet Marie.
2. Sweet Marie, list to me,
    Sweet Marie, list to me,
    I'm as thin as a Thomas cat, sweet Marie,
    But I've got the framework yet,
    So we'll be happy yet, you bet, sweet Marie.

SOURCE: *Inez Foster, 2515 E. 24th Street, Edwardsville, Illinois, November 1, 1949.*

"Down in Southern Illinois"

My father moved his family out of Southern Illinois because of his losing fight with malaria when I was a baby. During the next twenty years we lived in central Illinois where we gradually absorbed the idea that Southern Illinois was a poor place to live. I came back to teach in Southern Illinois in 1926, and after living here for more than thirty years I find that the words of the song, "Down in Southern Illinois" express my feelings very well.

1. You may sing of old Kentucky
    Or your Indiana home,
    You may boast of old Missouri
    Or the many lands you roam,
    But to me no land is dearer
    When I dream of girls and boys
    Than in the country of my childhood
    Down in Southern Illinois.
2. You may call it "Darkest Egypt,"
    You may call us green as grass,
    Say we live on mush and bacon,
    Johnny cakes and apple "sass,"
    But I tell you all your talking
    Don't begin to equal joys
    That I feel when in the country
    Down in Southern Illinois.

3. You may tell me of the grandeur
    Of big cities, oh so fine,
    You may say their life is better
    Than this country life of mine,
    But I dream of hogs and cattle,
    Country sights and lots of noise,
    And I guess I'd rather stay, Sir,
    Down in Southern Illinois.

SOURCE: *Evelyn Smith, New Burnside, Illinois, October 20, 1932.*

"Down in Old Franklin County"

Mr. M. C. Page, Newton, Illinois, gave me a version of this song on November 5, 1934, which included the first three verses only. Our source supplied us with the fourth verse.

"Down in Old Franklin County" sings a different song on life in the Illinois Ozarks. Compared to the pacific "feeling" of Saline County, which follows, this song of Franklin County exposes a more violent view of life in this part of the world.

It was down in Franklin County,
Where they never have the blues,
Where the Captain kills the Colonel,
And the Colonel kills the booze.

Where the horses they are pretty,
And the women they are too,
Where they kill men just for pastime
When there's nothing else to do.

Where you step out in the morning
Just to give your health a chance,
And you come home in the evening
With some buck-shot in your pants.

Where the owls won't hoot at nighttime
And the birds refuse to sing,
For it's Hell down in the boneyard
Where they shoot them on the wing.

SOURCE: *Beulah M. Douglas, 407 Mitchell Street, Benton, Illinois, April 3,
    1951.*

"County of Saline"

George T. Pratt, Hamburg, Illinois, wrote the words of the "County of Saline" in 1897. In this song, Mr. Pratt makes reference to the association with Egypt that Southern Illinois has taken on through the years. The link of the fertile plains of Egypt with those of Southern Illinois lies in the fact that Southern Illinois is enclosed on three sides by rivers: the Wabash River runs on the east side, the Mississippi River on the west, and the Ohio River on the south. Thus, the nickname that refers to Southern Illinois as "Little Egypt."

Mid the valleys and the hills,
Mid the woodlands and the rills,
In the land that pleasure fills
Is the County of Saline,
Is the County of Saline,
Is the County of Saline,
In the land that pleasure fills
Is the County of Saline.

Chorus: Grand old County of Saline,
Fertile spot of Egypt's plain,
True in days that thou has seen,
Still the County of Saline.

Broad and fertile are thy fields,
Great the income nature yields,
And the cause of right she shields
In the County of Saline,
In the County of Saline,
In the County of Saline,
And the cause of right she shields
In the County of Saline.

Homes and schools and churches, too,
And her people brave and true
Make the future bright in view
For the County of Saline,
For the County of Saline,
For the County of Saline,
Make the future bright in view
For the County of Saline.

SOURCE: *Mr. Kenneth Hale, Galatia, Illinois, November 2, 1948.*

2

Traditional Folk Songs

Unlike the songs in the preceding chapter, those included here are the Illinois Ozarks versions of songs that originated elsewhere. While the folk song, like any other type of song, is a means of communication, it differs from art song in the manner in which it is perpetuated, folk song being dependent upon oral tradition rather than the printed score. Because of his dependence upon learning by hearing rather than by seeing, the folk singer has no way to check his accuracy with reference to the tune, so changes occur, giving rise to a whole family of tune variants. The lyrics suffer fewer changes because many singers write the words down, as indicated by the many notebooks containing the lyrics of songs found among the folk singers of the Illinois Ozarks. This method of learning songs is still in use and will hopefully continue for a long time to come.

Our description of folk song does not cover all the songs that we feel should be included, nor does the following definition from the *Standard Dictionary of Folklore*:

> Like all other forms of verbal folk arts, such as the folktale and proverb, folk song is perpetuated by *oral tradition* . . .
>
> Although folk song is *perpetuated* by oral tradition, not all folk songs need to have *originated* in oral tradition and by folk creation. The discussions as to whether songs which are sung in a folk setting but come from the city are considered "true folk songs" are perhaps beside the point. Folk songs are best defined as songs which are current in the repertory of a folk group; the study of their origin is another matter.[1]

The songs included in this chapter were selected, for several reasons, from a long list collected from oral sources in the Illinois Ozarks. They are songs that people enjoyed singing. The emotional feeling of the songs is extremely varied. With the exception of "Old Pike," they are variants of songs found in many areas of the United States and show the kinship, through folk music, which people of the Illinois Ozarks have with all those about them. With the exception of "My Golden Ball" (Child 95),[2] we have omitted local versions of the traditional ballad as found in the Child collections. Our informants were usually older people who liked to sing and who remembered the songs popular among the folk of an earlier generation. Sometimes, however, the singers were younger people who had learned the songs from parents or friends. The informant for "My Golden Ball" gave this explanation:

> When I was just a kid and when I was in a rope swing out under the oak tree, I'd swing, swing, and sing this song. I thought it was terrible the way it began, you know. Well, you see, a boy was given this ball to take care of, and the king told him that if he lost it, he'd hang him, and the boy lost it and nobody found it. They had him out there ready to hang him up, and he'd beg every time when he'd see somebody else coming to wait till they got there to see if they'd found the ball. And they all gave up but the sweetheart and she didn't give up till she found it, and then she came with it and saved his life. That's what I thought was so wonderful, of course.[3]

Folk singers are not limited to the usual major and minor scales with the tunes ending on the first tone of the scale. In the song "Old Woman in Slab City," the tune ends on the fifth tone of the scale. The melody of "Little Mohee" is based on the Dorian scale or mode, D E F G A B C D. The use of the flat seventh in the songs "Old Grumbler" and "Old Pike" is characteristic of the mixolydian scale or mode, C D E F G A B-flat C. The rather curious ending of "The Sailor and the Maid," on the second tone of the scale, gives a feeling of continuing to the next verse, with no feeling of ending after each verse.

The simplicity of these songs and their ready adaptability to all sorts of environments are among the qualities that have given them a lasting appeal, particularly among people who, like our ancestors, had to supply their own entertainment. In *South Carolina Ballads*, Reed Smith sums up the varied history of "The Golden Ball" ("The Hangman's Tree," or "The Maid Freed from the Gallows"):

> In the game "The Golden Ball," the wheel of the ballad has come full circle. Composed before Chaucer's pilgrimage, sung in England and Scotland during the spacious times of Queen Elizabeth, recorded by the antiquarian scholar Bishop Thomas Percy in the

days of George III, . . . the ballad of "The Maid Freed from the Gallows" has in the end become a rustic English tale, a Negro cantefable in the Bahamas and the West Indies, a playlet at a Negro school commencement, and a children's game in the slums of New York City. A long life and a varied one.[4]

"KIND OLD HUSBAND"

This old song was obtained from the late Robert Wilson, a teacher at McLeansboro and many years county superintendent of schools of Hamilton County, who was a folk music man of the kind described by Professor Leach (*Ballad Book*): "One discovers that ballad singing and collecting run in families, that in a given community most of the people were listeners or at best participated only to the extent of singing the refrains, that keeping ballads alive was the business of the few, the few with a natural bent for singing and with a good memory for the old songs. Often such folk transmitted their talents and interest to their children." [5] Robert Wilson grew up in a pioneer family of this kind, from which he inherited a talent for singing folk songs and for playing the fiddle—as well as a large repertory of folk songs. In addition to "Kind Old Husband," Mr. Wilson recorded other songs of which John W. Allen and D. S. McIntosh recorded a number for the Library of Congress.

Vance Randolph has published three Ozark versions of "Kind Old Husband" in *Ozark Folksongs*.[6]

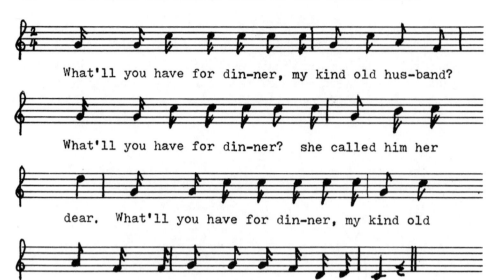

What'll you have for din-ner, my kind old hus-band?

What'll you have for din-ner? she called him her

dear. What'll you have for din-ner, my kind old

hus-band? The best old fel-low in the world.

Wife: What'll you have for dinner, my kind old husband?
           What'll you have for dinner? she called him her dear.
           What'll you have for dinner, my kind old husband?
           The best old fellow in the world.
Husband: Eggs. [*Spoken*]
Wife: How many will it take, my kind old husband?
           How many will it take? she called him her dear.
           How many will it take, my kind old husband?
           The best old fellow in the world.
Husband: Half a bushel. [*Spoken*]
Wife: That's enough to kill you, my kind old husband.
           That's enough to kill you, she called him her dear.
           That's enough to kill you, my kind old husband.
           The best old fellow in the world.
Husband: Just let 'em kill. [*Spoken*]
Wife: Where shall I bury you, my kind old husband?
           Where shall I bury you? she called him her dear.
           Where shall I bury you, my kind old husband?
           The best old fellow in the world.
Husband: In the chimney corner, where you always do. [*Spoken*]
Wife: Dogs'll scratch you up, my kind old husband.
           Dogs'll scratch you up, she called him her dear.
           Dogs'll scratch you up, my kind old husband.

The best old fellow in the world.

Husband: Just let 'em scratch. [*Spoken*]

Wife: Then I'll cry my eyes out, my kind old husband.

Then I'll cry my eyes out, she called him dear.

Then I'll cry my eyes out, my kind old husband.

The best old fellow in the world.

Husband: Cry your eyes out and go blind. [*Spoken*]

SOURCE: *Robert Wilson, Dahlgren, Illinois, October 12, 1933.*

"OLD WOMAN IN SLAB CITY"

The story in "Old Woman in Slab City" is approximately the same as that of a fairly widely distributed popular tale of trickery, a version of which may be found in Vance Randolph's *Who Blowed Up the Church House?*[7] Four other variants of this song collected in the Illinois Ozarks are entitled "Johnny Sands." Variants of "Johnny Sands" are also found in H. M. Belden's *Ballads and Songs*[8] and in A. C. Morris's *Folksongs of Florida*, as "The Old Woman in Ireland";[9] in W. A. Owens's *Swing and Turn*;[10] in L. J. Wolford's *The Play-Party in Indiana*, as "There Was an Old Woman in Ireland";[11] Charles Neely, *Tales and Songs of Southern Illinois*, has a version of "Johnny Sands" obtained in Belleville, Illinois.[12]

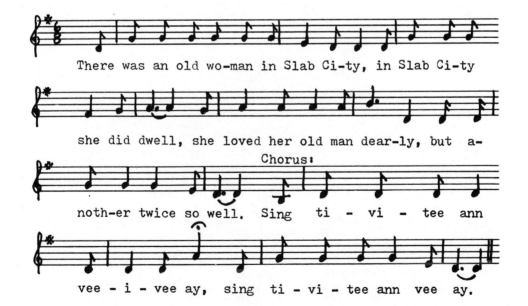

There was an old wo-man in Slab Ci-ty, in Slab Ci-ty she did dwell, she loved her old man dear-ly, but a-noth-er twice so well. Sing ti - vi - tee ann vee - i - vee ay, sing ti - vi - tee ann vee ay.

Chorus:

1. There was an old woman in Slab City,
   In Slab City she did dwell,
   She loved her old man dearly,
   But another twice so well.

Chorus:
   Sing ti-vi-tee ann`vee-i-vee ay,
   Sing ti-vi-tee ann vee ay.

2. Say's he, I'll go and drown myself,
   If I could find the way.
   Say's she, I'll go alongst with you,
   For fear you'd go astray.

3. They walked along, they charged along,
   Till they came to the river shore.
   Says he, my dear and loving wife,
   You'll have to push me o'er.

4. She stepped back a step or two,
   To run and push him in.
   He being nimble stepped aside,
   And headlong she went in.

5. And finding out her sad mistake,
   She began to scream and bawl.
   Says he, my dear and loving wife,
   I can't see you at all.

6. He being of good nature,
   And fearing she might swim,
   He got himself a great long pole,
   And pushed her further in.

7. And now my song is ended,
   And I can't sing any more,
   But wasn't she a great big fool,
   She never swum to shore.

SOURCE: *Bruce McLean from Wren Piper, Oakdale, Illinois, September 25, 1950.*

"LITTLE MOHEE"

There are five other versions of "Little Mohee" that were collected in the Illinois Ozarks and are similar except that the young sailor does not spend the night with the girl, and in three of them the young man decides to return to Little Mohee. This song is widely known all over the United States: "Its titles and variants are numerous, but in essence it is known all over the country from the mountains of the southeast, to the fishing towns of the northeast, and from the plains of the west, to the Pacific Islands." [13]

Charles Neely has two versions called "The Pretty Mohea" and "Mawee" [14] obtained in Harrisburg and Belleville respectively. There are also other variants: B. A. Arnold's *Folksongs of Alabama*, "Pretty Mohee"; [15] Morris [16] and Randolph, [17] "The Pretty Mohee"; and Dorothy Scaraborough, *A Song Catcher in the Southern Mountains*, [18] gives seven texts and one tune.

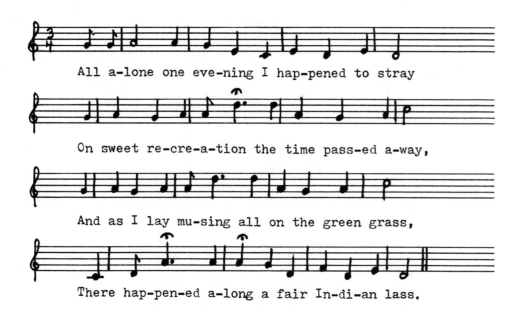

All a-lone one eve-ning I hap-pened to stray

On sweet re-cre-a-tion the time pass-ed a-way,

And as I lay mu-sing all on the green grass,

There hap-pen-ed a-long a fair In-di-an lass.

1.　All alone one evening I happened to stray
　　On sweet recreation the time passed away,
　　And as I lay musing all on the green grass,
　　There happened along a fair Indian lass.
2.　She sat down beside me and taking my hand,
　　She said, "You're a stranger and far from your land.
　　But now if you will, you are welcome to go,
　　For I live all alone in a neat little home."

3. The sun it was setting far over the sea,
    And as I went rambling with the lass of Mohee,
    We rambled and we roamed till we came to the cove,
    To a neat little cottage in a coconut grove.

4. All night there we tarried till dawn did appear,
    My ship it was ready, for home I must steer.
    O no, fondest creature, live here at your ease,
    And I'll teach you the language of the Island of Mohee.

5. O no fairest creature, that never shall be,
    I'll never more ramble far over the sea.
    For I have a sweetheart far out in the west,
    And I would not forsake her for all you possess.

6. Oh, now I'm at home and my friends round me stand.
    They try to console me by shaking my hand.
    But all they can do or all they can say,
    Is not to compare with the lass of Mohee.

SOURCE: *Henry Clay Lamp, Carmi, Illinois, April 13, 1949.*

"MY GOLDEN BALL"

"My Golden Ball" covers a familiar topic to ballads—the gallows. The man as victim is not unique, but is fairly rare. A second version of this ballad collected in the Illinois Ozarks has the young man as the gallows victim, and the mother, instead of the sweetheart, comes to the rescue in the last stanza. The informant said that she thought her mother, from whom she had learned the ballad, had changed the last stanza because she believed that a mother would stand by her boy when all others failed.

Many other versions of this song can be found: Arnold, "The Miller's Daughter"; [19] Belden, "The Maid Freed from the Gallows"; [20] Morris has four versions; [21] Owens, "The Hangman's Rope"; [22] Randolph, "Hold Your Hands, Old Man"; [23] Carl Sandburg, *The American Songbag*, "Hangman"; [24] MacEdward Leach, "The Golden Ball"; [25] and F. J. Child, "The Maid Freed from the Gallows." [26]

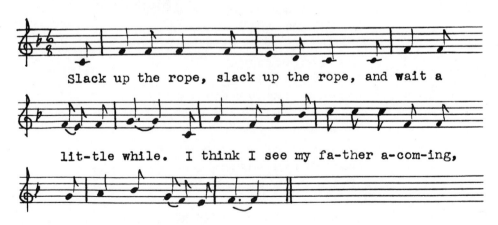

Slack up the rope, slack up the rope, and wait a

lit-tle while. I think I see my fa-ther a-com-ing,

out on that ro-ving wild.

1. Slack up the rope, slack up the rope,
   And wait a little while.
   I think I see my father a-coming,
   Out on that roving wild.

2. Father, have you found my golden ball,
   And have you come to set me free?
   Or have you come to see me hung,
   All on this linden tree?

3. I've not found your golden ball,
   And I've not come to set you free.
   But I have come to see you hung,
   Out on this linden tree.

4. Slack up the rope, slack up the rope,
   And wait a little while.
   I think I see my mother a-coming,
   Out on this roving wild.

5. Mother, have you found my golden ball,
   And have you come to set me free?
   Or have you come to see me hung,
   All on this linden tree.

6. I've not found your golden ball,
   And I've not come to set you free.
   But I have come to see you hung,
   Out on this linden tree.

7. Slack up the rope, slack up the rope,
   And wait a little while.
   I think I see my brother a-coming,
   Out on this roving wild.

8. Next, brother, have you found my golden ball,
   And have you come to set me free?
   Or have you come to see me hung,
   Out on this linden tree?

9. I've not found your golden ball,
   And I've not come to set you free.
   But I have come to see you hung,
   Out on this linden tree.

10. Slack up the rope, slack up the rope,
    And wait a little while.
    I think I see my sister a-coming,
    Out on this roving wild.

11. Sister, have you found my golden ball,
    And have you come to set me free?

Or have you come to see me hung,
Out on this linden tree?

12. I've not found your golden ball,
And I've not come to set you free.
But I have come to see you hung,
Out on this linden tree.

13. Slack up the rope, slack up the rope,
And wait a little while.
I think I see my true love coming,
Out on this roving wild.

14. True love, have you found my golden ball,
And have you come to set me free?
Or have you come to see me hung,
Out on this linden tree?

15. I have found your golden ball,
And I have come to set you free.
But I've not come to see you hung,
Out on this linden tree.

SOURCE: *Mrs. Lessie Parrish, Carbondale, Illinois, November 12, 1937.*

"IF YOU WANT TO GO A-COURTIN'"

"If You Want To Go A-Courtin'" tells of some of the hardships of "Courtin'."

Four versions of this song are found in Cecil J. Sharp's *English Folk Songs from the Southern Appalachians.*[27]

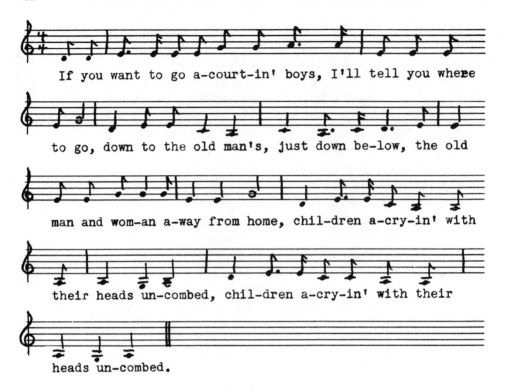

If you want to go a-court-in' boys, I'll tell you where

to go, down to the old man's, just down be-low, the old

man and wom-an a-way from home, chil-dren a-cry-in' with

their heads un-combed, chil-dren a-cry-in' with their

heads un-combed.

1. If you want to go a-courtin' boys,
    I'll tell you where to go,
    Down to the old man's just down below,
    The old man and woman gone away from home,
    Children a-cryin' with their heads uncombed,
    Children a-cryin' with their heads uncombed.

2. The old dirty duds a-hangin' on the loom,
    The old dirty floor and there ain't no broom,
    The old dirty dishes a-settin' on the shelf,
    If you want a clean plate boys, wash it up yourself,
    If you want a clean plate boys, wash it up yourself.

3. They asked me to eat and they thought I'd eat,
    Fell on me for to cut up the meat,
    The old dull knife and weren't no fork,
    Sawed about a half an hour and never made a mark,
    Sawed about a half an hour and never made a mark.

4. Sawed and I sawed and I sawed it out of the plate,
One of the girls says, "you'd better wait,"
Sawed and I sawed and I sawed it on the floor,
Gave the meat a kick and I sent it out the door,
Gave the meat a kick and I sent it out the door.

5. One of the girls says, "you'd better run,
For yander comes Dad with a double barrel gun,"
Stand my ground as brave as a bear,
Tangle my fingers in the old man's hair,
Tangle my fingers in the old man's hair.

SOURCE: *William Jones, Carbondale, Illinois, February 16, 1935.*

"OLD GRUMBLER"

"Old Grumbler" tells the woes a man can get when he trades his daily duties for his wife's. Another version collected in the Illinois Ozarks is entitled "Old Grandly."

Still other versions are to be found in Belden, "Father Grumbler"; [28] in Owens, "The Grumbler's Song"; [29] in Randolph, "Father Grumble"; [30] in Leach, "Father Grumble"; [31] and in the text from Louise Pound, "Traditional Ballads in Nebraska," *Journal of American Folklore.*[32]

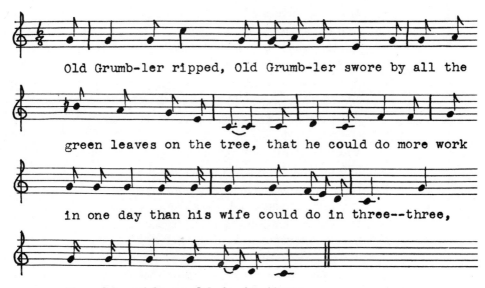

Old Grumb-ler ripped, Old Grumb-ler swore by all the

green leaves on the tree, that he could do more work

in one day than his wife could do in three--three,

than his wife could do in three.

1. Old Grumbler ripped, Old Grumbler swore
   By all the green leaves on the tree,
   That he could do more work in one day
   Than his wife could do in three—three,
   Than his wife could do in three.

2. Mis' Grumbler turned around about
   Saying, You'll have trouble now,
   For you may do the work in the house,
   And I'll go follow the plow—plow,
   And I'll go follow the plow.

3. And you must milk the muley cow
   For fear that she goes dry,
   And you must feed the pig in the pen,
   The pig that's blind in one eye—eye,
   The pig that's blind in one eye.

4. And you must watch the speckled hen
   For fear she lays astray,
   And you must spool the cut of thread
   That I spun yesterday—day,
   That I spun yesterday.

5. And you must churn the churning of cream
   That stands in yonder frame,
   And you must watch the kettle of mush
   For fear it catches a flame—flame,
   For fear it catches a flame.

6. Mis' Grumbler picked up the old ox goad
   And started to follow the plow,
   Old Grumbler picked the slop bucket up
   And started to milk the cow—cow,
   And started to milk the cow.

7. Old Muley kicked, Old Muley stomped,
   So, Muley, so—Old Muley kicked Old
   Grumbler's shins
   Till the blood ran down to his toes—toes,
   Till the blood ran down to his toes.

8. Next, Grumbler went to feed the pig,
   The pig that was blind in one eye,
   He bumped his head against the pen
   Till his brains were ready to fly—fly,
   Till his brains were ready to fly.

9. Next, Grumbler went to watch the hen
   For fear she laid astray,

But he forgot the cut of thread
That his wife spun yesterday—day,
That his wife spun yesterday.

10. Next Grumbler went to churn the cream
That stood in yonder frame,
But he forgot the kettle of mush
Till it was all in a flame—flame,
Till it was all in a flame.

11. Old Grumbler turned around about
To see how high the sun,
Old Grumbler ripped, Old Grumbler swore
That his wife would never come—come,
That his wife would never come.

12. Old Grumbler ripped, Old Grumbler swore
By all the green leaves on the tree,
If his wife didn't do a day's work in a year
She'll never be scolded by me—me,
She'll never be scolded by me.

SOURCE: *Mrs. Mono Jones, Sparta, Illinois, November 26, 1945.*

"THE SAILOR AND THE MAID"

"The Sailor and the Maid" is a song about the test of the faithfulness of true love. The maid's faithfulness is examined and rewarded in this song by her true lover.

When collecting this song, the informant said, "This song was taught to me by my father-in-law, Mr. D. L. Downey, of Hominy, Oklahoma. It was taught to him by his mother when they were living at Bellair, a small town near Casey, Illinois."

Another version collected in the Illinois Ozarks is entitled, "A Pretty Fair Maid." In this version, the returning lover is a soldier instead of a sailor. More versions can be found: Belden, "A Sweetheart in the Army"; [33] Morris, "Sailor's Return"; [34] Owens, "A Pretty Fair Maid"; [35] Randolph, "The Maiden in the Garden"; [36] Sandburg, "A Pretty Fair Maid"; [37] Scarborough has five texts and four tunes.[38]

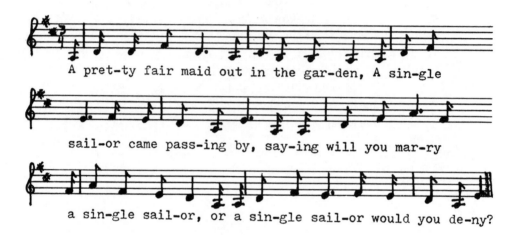

A pret-ty fair maid out in the gar-den, A sin-gle sail-or came pass-ing by, say-ing will you mar-ry a sin-gle sail-or, or a sin-gle sail-or would you de-ny?

1. A pretty fair maid out in the garden,
   A single sailor came passing by,
   Saying will you marry a single sailor,
   Or a single sailor would you deny?

2. Oh no said she, a man of honor,
   A man of honor you must be.
   How can ya impose upon a lady
   So worthy as your bride to be?

3. I have a true lover on the ocean,
   For seven long years he has been at sea,
   And if he should stay there seven years longer,
   No man on earth will marry me.

4. Perhaps your true lover he is wounded,
   Perhaps he is in some battle slain,
   Perhaps he to some fair girl married,
   And you may never see him again.

5. Perhaps my true lover he is wounded,
   Perhaps he is in some battle slain,
   Perhaps he to some fair girl married,
   I love the girl that married him.

6. He put his hand into his bosom,
   His fingers they were slim and small,
   And he drew forth a ring she'd given him,
   Prostrate before him she did fall.

7. He picked her up into his arms,
   And kisses gave her one two three,
   Saying will you marry a single sailor
   Who came so far to marry thee?

8. Her head inclined upon his shoulder,
   Her cheeks they grew like roses red,
   Saying I am thine forever, dear Willy,
   Till I am numbered with the dead.

SOURCE: *Geraldine Downey, Centralia, Illinois, January 6, 1949.*

"OLD PIKE"

"Old Pike" tells the story of the poor white who tries to better his lot by striking out to make it rich in the gold fields of California. But with the luck of the "pike," he loses what little he has on the way and is forced to return home with less than he started with.

In the 1850s and afterward, the word "pike(s)" had approximately the same connotation in California that "okie" had for a later generation. "Pike" was apparently first applied to persons from Pike County, Missouri, but was soon expanded to include all of Missouri and some neighboring territory: "A Pike in the California dialect is a native of Missouri, Arkansas, Northern Texas, or Southern Illinois." [39] The "old pike" of this song is probably a representative member of the Pike Clan, created after the pattern of the California myth.

This is the only version of this song that we have collected in this area, and it does not appear in any of the other collections that we have seen.

I once knew a man by the name of Pike, b'longed to the

fami-ly of Rigg-ins. And like an old fool he bought an

old mule and start-ed for the Cal-i-for-nia digg-ins.

Chorus:

Haul off your coat, roll up your sleeves, the plains

am a hard road to tra-vel. Haul off your coat, roll up

your sleeves, the plains am a hard road to tra-vel I be-

lieve.

1. I once knew a man by the name of Pike,
    B'longed to the family of Riggins.
    And like an old fool, he bought an old mule
    And started for the California diggins.

Chorus:

  Haul off your coat, roll up your sleeves,
  The plains am a hard road to travel.
  Haul off your coat, roll up your sleeves,
  The plains am a hard road to travel I believe.

2. He loaded his mule with bacon and beans,
    Hardtack, tobacco, and whiskey.
    He would-a took more, but the mule was too pore,
    It made the old fellow feel risky.

3. He traveled on through the mud and mire,
    Till he came to old Platte river.
    There he went to swim across, the mule was lost,
    And away went his bacon forever.

4. Old Pike swam out like a half-drowned rat,
    Minus of his boots and his britches.
    He turned for home, his good mule gone,
    And all for the California riches.

SOURCE: *Annamae Todd, Pinckneyville, Illinois, April 24, 1951.*

"FROG WENT A-COURTING"

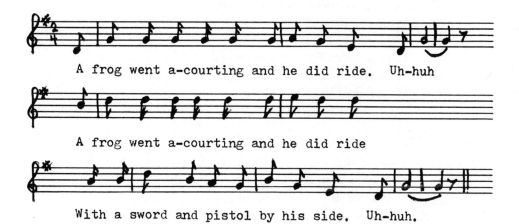

A frog went a-courting and he did ride. Uh-huh

A frog went a-courting and he did ride

With a sword and pistol by his side. Uh-huh.

"Frog Went A-Courting" is one of the most popular of folk songs: "Innumerable variants occur in oral tradition all over the United States among both Negro and white singers, and in England, Ireland, Scotland, and Wales." [40] Twenty-seven informants contributed their versions of "Frog Went A-Courting" to our collection.

Some other versions are, Arnold; [41] Belden; [42] Morris has seven versions; [43] Owens; [44] Randolph, "The Frog's Courtship"; [45] Sandburg; [46] Scarborough has three texts and two tunes. [47]

1. A frog went a-courting and he did ride. Uh-huh.
   A frog went a-courting and he did ride.
   With a sword and a pistol by his side. Uh-huh.

2. He rode up to Miss Mousie's door. Uh-huh.
   He rode up to Miss Mousie's door,
   He hit so hard that he made it roar. Uh-huh.

3. Miss Mousie asked him to come in. Uh-huh.
   Miss Mousie asked him to come in,
   The way they courted was a sin. Uh-huh.

4. He took Miss Mousie on his knee. Uh-huh.
   He took Miss Mousie on his knee
   And said, "Miss Mousie, will you marry me?" Uh-huh.

5. "Before, Kind Sir, I can answer that. Uh-huh.
   Before, Kind Sir, I can answer that,
   I'll have to ask my Uncle Rat." Uh-huh.

6. Uncle Rat gave his consent. Uh-huh.
   Uncle Rat gave his consent,
   The weasel wrote the publishment. Uh-huh.

7. Uncle Rat he went to town. Uh-huh.
   Uncle Rat he went to town
   To buy his niece a wedding gown. Uh-huh.

8. What did he get for a wedding gown? Uh-huh.
   What did he get for a wedding gown?
   Piece of hide of an old gray hound. Uh-huh.

9. Where shall the wedding supper be? Uh-huh.
   Where shall the wedding supper be?
   Away down yonder in a hollow tree. Uh-huh.

10. What shall the wedding supper be? Uh-huh.
    What shall the wedding supper be?
    Two red beans and a black-eyed pea. Uh-huh.

11. First came in was a bumble-bee. Uh-huh.
    First came in was a bumble-bee
    With his banjo on his knee. Uh-huh.

12. Next came in was a big black cat. Uh-huh.
    Next came in was a big black cat
    To put a stop to all of that. Uh-huh.

13. Miss Mousie went skipping across the wall. Uh-huh
    Miss Mousie went skipping across the wall
    Her foot it slipped and she got a fall. Uh-huh.

14. So this poor frog was made a wid'er. Uh-huh
    So this poor frog was made a wid'er
    He swore by all he'd have another. Uh-huh.

15. There's pen and ink all on the shelf. Uh-huh
    There's pen and ink all on the shelf
    If you want any more you can write it yourself. Uh-huh.

SOURCE: *Robert Wilson, Dahlgren, Illinois, October 8, 1941. Verses 5, 6, 7, and 8 were taken from a version sung by Miss Virdell Krewinghaus, Venedy, Illinois, in February 1947.*

"DURIE DOWN"

"Durie Down" gives a humorous account of a traveler who finds that things are better back where he came from—in good ole Illinois.

1. Come all ye young people I pray you draw near,
   A comical story you soon shall hear,
   A comical ditty to you I'll unfold,
   I came from Missouri at twenty years old.
   Durie down, down, down durie down.

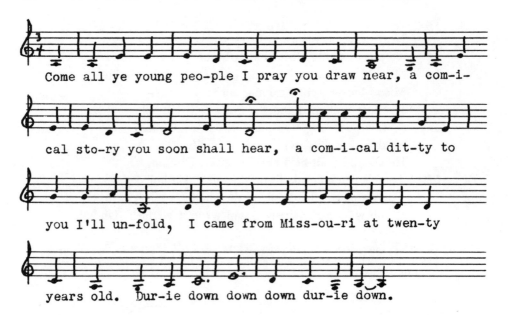

Come all ye young peo-ple I pray you draw near, a com-i-

cal sto-ry you soon shall hear, a com-i-cal dit-ty to

you I'll un-fold, I came from Miss-ou-ri at twen-ty

years old. Dur-ie down down down dur-ie down.

2. I stopped at a tavern to stay all night,
My supper and breakfast I thought it alright,
The table was set and the nicknacks were spread
With hoecake and hominy and possum's head.
Durie down, down, down durie down.

3. Now all the good people were heartily fed
On hoecake and hominy and possum's head,
The straw it was scattered, the sheep skin was spread,
Now says the old woman we'll all go to bed.
Durie down, down, down durie down.

4. I laid myself down expecting some ease,
I scarcely could sleep for the lice and the fleas,
The fleas they would bite and the lice they would crawl,
It's enough to torment any human at all.
Durie down, down, down durie down.

5. Adieu to Missouri, I'll bid you farewell,
Go back to Illinois where I used to dwell,
Where the women are rarin' and tearin' their hair
For the loss of their true love since I left there.
Durie down, down, down durie down.

SOURCE: *Mrs. Clyde Brown, Springertown, Illinois, October 9, 1952, by Mrs. Ester C. Harris of Fairfield, Illinois.*

Part 2

Play— Party Games

INTRODUCTION

Traditionally singing games or play-party games were played at home gatherings. The participants, both young and old, were friends of the family. Unlike the traditional square dances, many of the games permit any number of persons to play. Weather allowing, the games were played outside on the lawn. Otherwise, the largest room in the house was used. The games included practically all the figures of the "square" dance, such as: grand right and left, do-si-do (dos à dos), swing, circle left, right hands across, left hands back, both hands across, ladies bow and gents bow under, circle left, and swing like thunder. Unlike the square dance where the music was supplied by instruments such as the fiddle, guitar, and banjo, the play-party game songs were sung by the dancers themselves. One informant told me that in the group she played with, it was considered bad taste for the girls to sing, that the young men had that responsibility. I do not believe that this was the general practice, however. Usually there was a definite leader in the group who set the tempo and cued the words.

The first play-party that I attended was held in the basement of a country home near Carbondale, Illinois. The host directed the games and taught the songs to all the guests, who were adults. Since the games were new to the group, only a few were played. This event occurred more than twenty years ago before I began to be interested in collecting singing games, so I did not set the tunes or words down. I do remember that we played a Virginia Reel, and for the last part we sang as we cast off and went under the arch:

> Shew rabbi shew shew, shew rabbi shew
> Shew rabbi shew shew, shew rabbi shew.

My mama told me long time ago
Never to marry no girls below.

No girls below boys, no girls below
Never to marry no girls below.

(I've often wondered just who were these girls below?)

The games included in this part were all collected in the Illinois Ozarks and each game has complete directions for playing. The terms "play-party game" and "singing game" are used interchangeably.

TERMS USED IN SINGING GAMES

CONTRA OR LONGWAYS.   Two lines of players face each other, with the ladies on one side and the gentlemen on the other side, opposite their partners.

DOUBLE CIRCLE.   Partners face counterclockwise, with the ladies on the outside of the circle, and the gentlemen on the inside.

SINGLE CIRCLE.   All face toward the center in single file; the ladies stand to the right of their partners.

SQUARE SET.   Four couples make up each set. Couple one is nearest the source of the music with the other couples numbered to the right around the set.

ACTIONS AND FIGURES

ALLEMANDE LEFT.   The gentleman turns to the lady on the left (his corner), the lady turns to the gentleman on the right (her corner); they join left hands, turn once around, and return to place.

DO-SI-DO NO. 1.   Each gentleman joins left hands with his partner and turns her once around; he then joins right hands with the opposite lady and turns her once around; then he joins left hands with his partner and turns her around so that she is standing on his right.

DO-SI-DO NO. 2.   The gentleman and lady move forward to meet each other, pass each other by the right shoulders, sidestep behind each other, moving backward, they pass each other by the left shoulders to their original positions.

GRAND RIGHT AND LEFT.   Partners face each other and join right hands. Gentlemen face counterclockwise and ladies face clockwise. As all move forward, partners drop right hands, join left hands with the next person, join right hands with the next person and so on weaving around the circle until they reach their partners.

ONCE AND A HALF SWING.   This call usually comes after the grand right and left and indicates that each gentleman should swing his partner once around and then swing each lady in turn as all move forward like the grand right and left, but with a turn. Gentlemen move counterclockwise around the circle.

PROMENADE.   Couples hold hands, as in the skating position, and march in a counterclockwise direction around the circle.

REEL.   The reel, which is done in contra formation, usually starts after the head couple slide-steps to the foot and back to the head of the formation. The head couple joins right hands and turns once and a half around. The girl goes to the second boy and the boy to the second girl, then each new couple joins left hands and turns around. The head couple then meets in the center and turns by the right hand. The head couple now goes to the third girl and boy and turns by the left, then back in the center by the right, and so on down the set.

SWING.   This is done in several ways: 1. The usual ballroom position where partners face each other, the gentleman joining left hand with lady's right hand, placing his right arm around lady's waist with the lady placing her left hand over the gentleman's left shoulder just below the back of the neck. Partners stand as far apart as this position will allow, for the two-step is done while the couple turns to the left, so there must be as much freedom as possible for the feet to move. 2. The hands join, gentleman's left hand to lady's right hand and gentleman's right hand to lady's left hand—or, instead of joining hands, they can grasp each other's arms above the elbows. Always turn to the left.

TWO-STEP.   The basic step in Middle West traditional singing games— done to 2/4 meter—is executed by stepping forward on the left foot on the count of one, sliding the right foot up to the heel a little to the right of the left foot on the second half of count one, then forward with left foot on count of two. The next measure starts on the right foot and repeats.

3

Singing Games: Contra Formation

Judging by the number of singing games to be played in contra or longways, this activity was very popular in the Illinois Ozarks. Additional games played in contra formation, found in this area are: "Boston Girls," "Chase the Squirrel," "Going to the Party," "Michigan Girls," "Paw-Paw Patch," "Buffalo Gals," "John I'll Tell Your Daddy," "Molly Brooks," "Hog and Hominy," "Shoot the Buffalo," and "Old Brass Wagon."

The first game in this section, "Rosabeckaliner," is a fast reel. "Weevily Wheat" served as music for the Virginia Reel and, also, gave the players a chance to "kid" each other through the verses. "Said the Blackbird" obviously had a dual purpose, first, the dance itself and second, the learning of the alphabet.

"ROSABECKALINER"

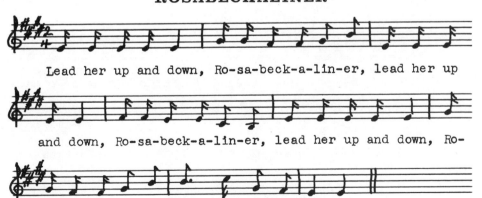

Lead her up and down, Ro-sa-beck-a-lin-er, lead her up

and down, Ro-sa-beck-a-lin-er, lead her up and down, Ro-

sa-beck-a-lin-er, won't you be my dar-ling?

2. Change and swing, Rosabeckaliner,
   Change and swing, Rosabeckaliner,
   Change and swing, Rosabeckaliner,
   Won't you be my darling?
3. Gee, ho, haw, Beck and Diner,
   Gee, ho, haw, Beck and Diner,
   Gee, ho, haw, Beck and Diner,
   Won't you be my darling?
4. Wheel about, whirl about, Rosabeckaliner,
   Wheel about, whirl about, Rosabeckaliner,
   Wheel about, whirl about, Rosabeckaliner,
   Won't you be my darling?

SOURCE: *Miss Frances Lee Whiteside, Chester, Illinois, March 6, 1945.*

Formation: Contra, with not more than five or six couples, and the ladies in one line and the gentlemen in the other.

Action: The head couple slide-steps to the foot of the set and back to the head of the set during the singing of the first verse.

During the singing of the remaining verses, the head couple reels to the foot of the set, where they remain. The second couple leads out as the song is repeated.

For other versions of "Rosabeckaliner," see Vance Randolph's *Ozark Folksongs* [1] and Jean Thomas and Joseph A. Leeder's *Singin' Gatherin'*.[2]

"WEEVILY WHEAT"

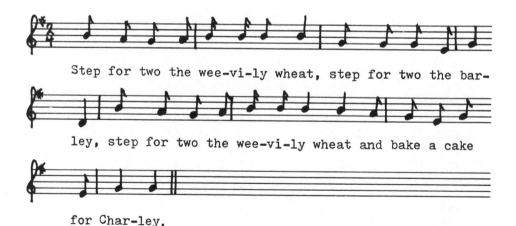

Step for two the wee-vi-ly wheat, step for two the bar-
ley, step for two the wee-vi-ly wheat and bake a cake
for Char-ley.

1. Step for two the weevily wheat,
   Step for two the barley,
   Step for two the weevily wheat
   And bake a cake for Charley.

2. Right hand round the weevily wheat,
   Right hand round the barley,
   Right hand round the weevily wheat
   And bake a cake for Charley.

3. Left hand round the weevily wheat,
   Left hand round the barley,
   Left hand round the weevily wheat
   And bake a cake for Charley.

4. Two hands round the weevily wheat,
   Two hands round the barley,
   Two hands round the weevily wheat
   And bake a cake for Charley.

5. Over the hill we skip together,
   So early in the morning,
   Hark at hand as here we stand
   As truly as two lovers.

6. If you love me as I love you,
   We'll have no time to tarry,
   We'll have the old folks fixing round
   For you and I to marry.

7. Do you think I'd marry the likes of you
   Do you think I'd marry my cousin
   Why, I can get such girls as you
   For forty cents a dozen.

8. If you can get such girls as me
   For forty cents a dozen,
   You had better buy a whole carload
   And ship them over to Boston.

SOURCE: *Lloyd Sager, Noble, Illinois, April 3, 1952.*

Formation: Contra with the girls in one line and the boys in the other. Each set should be limited to six girls and six boys.

Action:

Verse 1:   The head girl and foot boy go forward and curtsy or bow. The opposites do the same.

Verse 2:   Right hand around.

Verse 3:   Left hand around.

Verse 4:   Two hands around.

Verse 5:   The head couple skips to the foot of the set and back to the head of the set.

Verses 6–8:   The head couple reels to the foot of the set where they remain and the game is repeated with a new head couple.

Other versions of "Weevily Wheat" are available: Richard Chase, *Old Songs and Singing Games*;[3] William A. Owens, *Swing and Turn*;[4] M. Katherine Price, *The Source Book of Play-Party Games*;[5] and Randolph has six versions in *Ozark Folksongs*.[6]

"SAID THE BLACKBIRD"

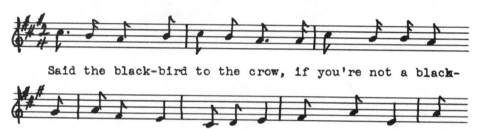

Said the black-bird to the crow, if you're not a black-

bird, I don't know.   Ev-er since you've been born, you've

been ac-cused of pull-ing up corn.   A B C D E F G   H I

J K L M N O P, L M N O P Q R S T U V, W X Y and Z.

SOURCE: *Mr. and Mrs. John Golder, Rural Route, Carlyle, Illinois, May 6, 1947.*

Formation: Contra, with the girls in one line and the boys in the other.

Action: Each couple reels, as in the Virginia Reel, to the foot of the set.

4

Singing Games: Single Circle Formation

The action in the single circle games is very closely related to the figures in the traditional square dances.

"Goin' upon the Mountain" was popular with the courtin' age. One charming lady told me that the young folks would meet at some crossroads and dance these games in the moonlight. With a chuckle she said she wondered what people would think nowadays if they saw this sort of thing at some highway intersection. Such phrases as "my darling girl" and "every girl that's here tonight is sweeter than honeycomb" served the boys well.

When "Oh Sister Phoebe" was played, any girl afraid of being kissed was sure to drop out, as the whole purpose of the game was to give the boys an excuse to choose and kiss any girl in the game. The contest for the hat gave the boys a chance for a bit of rough-and-tumble play.

"Susan Brown" by contrast is a very dignified game with no close contact. The "do-si-do," "right hands across," and "circle left" were approved activities by most of the religious folks who generally objected to the kissing games and the close body swing.

How such words and phrases as "ti-de-o," "jingle Joe," and "fling-daddle-doodle-daddle," are "come by" is a mystery. The various versions of "Ti-De-O" found in the area always are identified by this title.

The version of "Uncle Johnny Sick in Bed" that is presented makes no mention of Johnny kissing Mr. Jones's daughter, but as played by young folks, this was the climax of the game. As these games have been adapted for children, such adult ideas are generally deleted.

"GOIN' UPON THE MOUNTAIN"

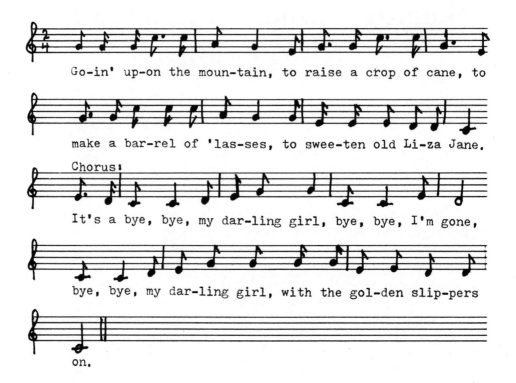

Go-in' up-on the moun-tain, to raise a crop of cane, to

make a bar-rel of 'las-ses, to swee-ten old Li-za Jane.

Chorus:

It's a bye, bye, my dar-ling girl, bye, bye, I'm gone,

bye, bye, my dar-ling girl, with the gol-den slip-pers

on.

2.   I used to ride the old gray horse,
But now I ride the roan,
You may court your own true love,
But you'd better leave mine alone. [*Chorus*]

3.   Meat's on the goose's foot,
The marrow's in the bone,
Every girl that's here tonight
Is sweeter than honeycomb. [*Chorus*]

4.   I used to make my living
By railroad and steam,
But now I make my living
By high low Jack, and the game. [*Chorus*]

SOURCE: *Mrs. Thelma Whittington, Whittington, Illinois, January 5, 1949.*

Formation: Single circle of partners.

Action:

Verse 1:   Players circle to the left.

Chorus: Each gentleman swings his corner, then swings his partner, then all do the grand right and left.

When partners meet, they turn back with a grand right and left.

When partners next meet, they do a two-arm swing on around the circle, swinging each lady in turn, until they meet their partners again, then all promenade counterclockwise.

The song is sung through from the beginning to the end, but if the action is not completed, the verses are repeated or new ones are improvised.

"OH SISTER PHOEBE"

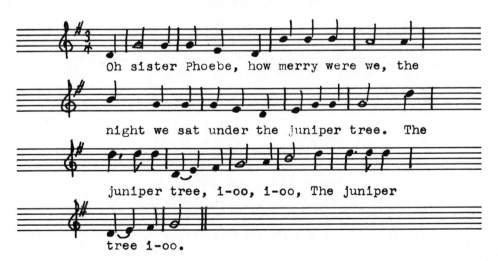

Oh sister Phoebe, how merry were we, the

night we sat under the juniper tree. The

juniper tree, i-oo, i-oo, The juniper

tree i-oo.

2. Put this hat on your head, keep your head warm,
    Take a sweet kiss, it'll do you no harm.
    But a great deal of good, I'm sure, I'm sure,
    But a great deal of good I'm sure.

SOURCE: *Roberta Morris, Centralia, Illinois, October 21, 1948.*

Formation: Single circle, with a gentleman in the center. A hat is on the floor in the center of the circle.

Action: During the singing of the first verse, the circle moves clockwise and the gentleman in the center chooses a lady from the circle and brings her into the center with him. On the first line of the second verse, the lady picks up the hat and puts it on the gentleman's head. He takes it off and kisses her, then puts the hat back on the floor in the center of the circle. At the end of the second verse, all gentlemen in the circle try to get the hat. The gentleman who succeeds is the new gentleman in the center. He places the hat on the floor and the game is repeated.

For another version of this song entitled "Old Sister Phoebe," see Leah J. Wolford's *The Play-Party in Indiana*.[1]

"SUSAN BROWN"

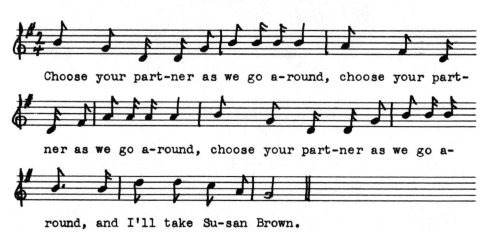

Choose your part-ner as we go a-round, choose your part-ner as we go a-round, choose your part-ner as we go a-round, and I'll take Su-san Brown.

2. Four hands up in a pokey whirl,
    Four hands up in a pokey whirl,
    Four hands up in a pokey whirl,
    I love you Susan Brown.

3. Change and swing waltzing swing,
    Change and swing waltzing swing,
    Change and swing waltzing swing,
    And I'll take Susan Brown.

4. Fare thee well my dear little Miss,
    Fare thee well my dear little Miss,
    Fare thee well my dear little Miss,
    And good-bye Susan Brown.

SOURCE: *Ina Setzekorn, Nashville, Illinois, February 4, 1947.*

Formation: A circle of partners with an extra couple in the center.

Action: During the singing of the first verse, the players in the circle dance in the clockwise direction, while the couple in the center each chooses a partner.

During the singing of the second verse the players in the circle dance in the counterclockwise direction, while the couples in the center cross right hands in a star and circle in the clockwise direction.

During singing of third verse the two couples in the center swing.

During the singing of the fourth verse the players in the outer circle stand still, while the two couples in the center execute the do-si-do number one.

As the game is repeated, the couple that started the game in the center joins the circle, and the couple chosen by the first couple remains in the center.

Leah Wolford has a version of this song entitled, "Cuckoo Waltz." [2]

"TI-DE-O"

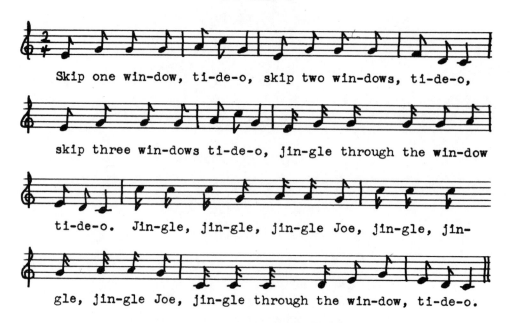

Skip one win-dow, ti-de-o, skip two win-dows, ti-de-o,

skip three win-dows ti-de-o, jin-gle through the win-dow

ti-de-o. Jin-gle, jin-gle, jin-gle Joe, jin-gle, jin-

gle, jin-gle Joe, jin-gle through the win-dow, ti-de-o.

SOURCE: *Thelma Brame, RR 2, Salem, Illinois, who learned the game from Mrs. Ralph Helpinstine, RR 2, Centralia, Illinois, and gave it to me on December 9, 1948.*

Formation: Single circle of partners.

Action: The girls stand still. The boys weave in and out in a counterclockwise direction, past one girl, past two girls, past three girls, then swing the fourth girl. During the singing of the last four measures all the boys promenade in the counterclockwise direction with the fourth girl.

To vary the game, the girls may weave in and out as the boys stand still.

The informant told us that this was the way the game was played around Tennessee Prairie which is near Centralia, Illinois. For other versions of this song see: Wolford, *The Play-Party in Indiana*; [3] Owens, *Swing and Turn*; [4] Price, *The Source Book of Play-Party Games*; [5] Randolph, *Ozark Folksongs*,[6] and under the title, "Toddy-O," Mrs. L. D. Ames has a version in "The Missouri Play-Party," in the *Journal of American Folklore.*[7]

"UNCLE JOHNNY SICK IN BED"

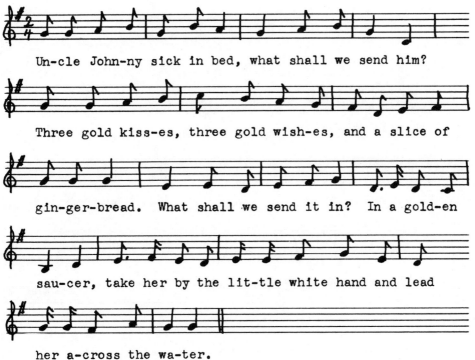

Un-cle John-ny sick in bed, what shall we send him?

Three gold kiss-es, three gold wish-es, and a slice of

gin-ger-bread. What shall we send it in? In a gold-en

sau-cer, take her by the lit-tle white hand and lead

her a-cross the wa-ter.

2. Doctor, doctor, can you tell what will make poor Johnny well?
   He is sick and 'bout to die, and that would make poor Mary cry.
   Mary's here and Mary's there, and Mary's on the water,
   Johnny's got the prettiest girl of Mr. Jones's daughters.

SOURCE: *Marie Patton, RFD 3, Marissa, Illinois, June 24, 1948.*

Formation: Single circle with Johnny squatting in the center.

Action: All join hands and circle to the left. When the group sings "take her by her little white hand," Johnny chooses a girl and takes her to the center.

All stand still doing the singing of the second verse.

As the game is repeated, the chosen one takes the place of Johnny in the circle.

Our informant told us that she learned this game in a rural school in Washington County, near Marissa, Illinois. In Wolford's *The Play-Party in Indiana*,[8] he cites only the text.

"GOIN' DOWN TO CAIRO"

Go-in' down to Cai-ro, good-bye and a good-bye, go-in'

down to Cai-ro, good-bye Li-za Jane.   Black them boots

and make them shine, good-bye and a good-bye, black them

boots and make them shine, good-bye Li-za Jane.

Version of the tune from Velma Reynolds

Go-in' down to Cai-ro, to Cai-ro, to Cai-ro, go-in'

down to Cai-ro, good-bye Li-za Jane.

1A. Goin' down to Cairo,
      Good-bye and a good-bye,
      Goin' down to Cairo,
      Good-bye Liza Jane.

1B. Black them boots and make them shine,
      Good-bye and a good-bye,
      Black them boots and make them shine,
      Good-bye Liza Jane.

2A.   Oh, how I love her,
      And ain't that a shame,
      Oh, how I love her,
      Good-bye Liza Jane.

2B.   I ain't got time to kiss you now,
      I'm sorry, I'm sorry,
      I ain't got time to kiss you now,
      I'm sorry Liza Jane.

SOURCE: *Lorena H. Webster, 2112 Division street, Murphysboro, Illinois, April 27, 1951.*

Formation: Single circle of about eight couples.

Action: During the singing of 1A the entire circle of players dance, doing a foot-stamping two-step, in the clockwise direction, single file. At 1B all gentlemen turn around to face their partner and all do the grand right and left, until partners are met. Then each gentleman swings each lady in turn until he reaches his partner again, this time swinging her twice around. All promenade until the end of the verse being sung at the time.

The song is sung straight through from beginning to end. If the action is not completed, the song is repeated.

Variations in the actions include the following: When the leader shouts, "Cairo," the action is immediately reversed.

"Goin' Down to Cairo" originated in the Illinois Ozarks. The Cairo in the title is the city located above the juncture of the Ohio and Mississippi rivers in Illinois. The following story about the game was obtained from Mr. R. B. Shelton by Mr. George O. Rice of Joppa, Illinois, December 10, 1947.

> I am not at all sure of the year, but I think it must have been about the year of 1858 that my mother and I stood looking at the field of tobacco which had been killed by the frost in the last part of August. This was to have been our only income, for my father had died a few years ago. I shall never forget the look of pain and frightened expression on my mother's face. It seemed as though practically all the corn and tobacco in this part of the country had been lost. It seemed as though the crops south of the Ohio River had not been damaged very much, so a few of the planters sent their crops up the river to Cairo and people all over the country came to Cairo to buy provisions. Several of the men would journey down to

Cairo and many times would arrive before the men came in with the cargo and would wait several days. It was pretty hard to find a good place to pass the time away so they began going to the saloons and various other places where they were entertained. The women noticed on the return trips that the men "blacked their boots" and dressed up a great deal more than usual and began to make frequent trips to Cairo. Many fabulous tales were told about the men having a "Liza Jane" that they were interested in. As a result of this, many of the women began going with their husbands, and the manner of entertainment was somewhat changed. Parties and games were played which usually wound up in a square dance. The game, "Goin' Down to Cairo" was first played there as a joke, but it was well-liked and the people brought it back with them. I remember that this was one of the favorite games when I was a boy.

Of the fifteen versions collected in the area, all have essentially the same tune, except the one from Velma Reynolds which is presented with the more usual tune to show the difference.

There is considerable variation in the words and some additional verses. The second phrase, "Good-bye and a good-bye," appears as "Get along, get along," or "To Cairo, to Cairo," or "Good-bye and a bye-bye." "Black them boots and make them shine," is the same in all versions, however the line that follows it, "Good-bye and a good-bye," changes to "And-ah, howdy," or "Howdy, howdy," or "And howdy and howdy," and "Get along, get along."

The second verse 2A is changed in the Kimmel [9] version to:

> Once and a half as we go around,
> Git along, git along,
> Once and a half as we go around,
> Git along Liza Jane.

The second verse 2A and 2B is changed in the Jordan [10] version to:

> 2A. Goin' away to leave you,
> And good-bye and good-bye,
> Goin' away to leave you,
> And a good-bye Liza Jane.
>
> 2B. Had no hat and had no rim,
> And good-bye and good-bye,
> Had no hat and had no rim,
> And a good-bye Liza Jane.

In an additional third verse, 3B follows the repetition of verse 2A and 3A:

> 3B. Harness up the yellow mule,
> Curry down his mane,
> Throw the bridle over his head,
> And go see Liza Jane.

The second verse 2B is changed in the Boston [11] version to:

> I'll be yours if you'll be mine,
> In the good-bye and the bye-bye,
> I'll be yours if you'll be mine,
> Good-bye Liza Jane.

The second verse 2A is changed in the Trainer [12] version to:

> Oh, she died and how I cried,
> Good-bye and good-bye,
> Oh, she died and how I cried,
> Good-bye Liza Jane.

The second verse 2B is changed in the Briley [13] version to:

> The Old Cow died and how I cried,
> Good-bye and-a-bye-bye,
> The old cow died and how I cried,
> Good-bye Liza Jane.

There is an additional verse 3A in the Briley version.

> 3A. Promenade on the inside ring
> Good-bye and-a-bye-bye,
> Promenade on the inside ring,
> Good-bye Liza Jane.

The third verse 3A and 3B is added in the Lockard [14] version.

> 3A. She went up the new cut road,
> And I went down the lane,
> Hung my foot in a holler stump,
> And out jumped Liza Jane.
> 3B. Run along home Liza,

> Good gal, good gal,
> Run along home Liza,
> Run along Liza Jane.

Occasionally verse 3A was changed to:

> 3A. We met on the mountain,
> We met on the train,
> Run along Liza good gal,
> Run along Liza Jane.

The second verse 2A is changed in the Gayer [15] version to:

> 2A. I ain't got time to kiss you now,
> But I'll hug you, hug you,
> Ain't got time to kiss you now,
> Good-bye Liza Jane.

The third verse 3A and 3B is as follows in the Reynolds [16] version:

> 3A. Going down to Rousters,
> To Rousters, to Rousters,
> Going down to Rousters,
> To get some lager beer.
>
> 3B. A rough old road and sorry team
> Good-bye and bye-bye
> A rough old road and a sorry team
> Good-bye Liza Jane.

The second verse 2A and 3A are changed in the Gholson [17] version to:

> 2A. Where you going Liza?
> Get along, get along.
> Where you going Liza?
> Get along Liza Jane.
>
> 3A. What you going to name the baby?
> Get along, get along.
> What you going to name the baby?
> Get along Liza Jane.

The remaining six versions collected in the Illinois Ozarks contain no additional phrases or verses.

5

Singing Squares

The singing square dances were adaptations of the traditional square-dance figures. Instead of a caller directing the dance above the background of instrumental music, the dancers went through the figures mostly without prompting.

"Build a Brick House" was often used as a singing game for any number of players, as the number was limited only by the size of the room. Here it is set up for eight dancers. The traditional square-dance call for this figure went something like this:

> First couple out to the couple on the
> right. Circle left. Right hands across
> and circle left. Left hands back. Both
> hands across. Ladies bow, the gents bow
> under, circle left, and swing like thunder.

"The Girl I Left behind Me" was very popular as a singing game, and also as a fiddle tune. The third verse of this version was used as the first verse of the singing game, the action conforming to the words. The second verse of the singing game used for the promenade usually went like this:

> Oh that girl, that pretty little girl,
> That girl I left behind me,
> I'll weep and sigh till the day I die,
> For the girl I left behind me.

The words for "Molly Brooks" gives directions for the figure of the dance, except for the circle left which is done as the first verse is sung. The head couple executes the figure with each couple in turn. The figure is similar to that done in "Build a Brick House" except that the players, after the "right hands across and left hands back," swing first the opposite, then their own, then move on to the next couple.

The square-dance call, "First Old Gent," is typical of the traditional calls in the Illinois Ozarks. The modern or recent square-dance records demand complicated maneuvers that permit no time for "cutting up" or "showing off" as is called for in this dance. To see one "old gent" out in the center doing a solo dance, as the others urge him on, is a treat that few modern square dancers have experienced.

"BUILD A BRICK HOUSE"

I went down town to build a brick house, to get a pail

of wa-ter, threw one arm a-round the old man, the oth-er

a-round his daugh-ter.

Chorus:
Fare you well my darling girl,
Fare you well she's gone,
Fare you well my darling girl,
With the golden slippers on her.
2. I went down town to build a brick house
Fourteen stories high.
Every room that I was in
Was lined with punkin pie.

SOURCE: *Mr. Lloyd Sager, Flora, Illinois, 1952.*

Formation: Single circle of couples.

Action:

Verse 1:   During the singing of the first line, the head couple joins hands in a circle with the second couple.

During the second line the ladies join both hands, and the gentlemen join both hands, with the ladies' hands below the hands of the gentlemen.

During the third line the gentlemen raise their arms over the heads of the ladies.

During the fourth line the ladies raise their arms over the heads of the gentlemen.

Chorus: During the first two lines of the chorus all drop hands and gentlemen swing with their corner ladies.

During the last two lines of the chorus the gentlemen swing with their partners.

This action is repeated as the second verse is sung, and the head couple goes on to the next couple. As soon as the head couple has reached the fourth couple, the second couple begins the dance with the third couple. Each couple in turn begins dancing as soon as the couple to their right is free to dance, after the leaders have passed. As soon as the couples reach their starting place they remain there to dance with the advancing couples.

For a slightly different tune on "Build a Brick House," different directions, and similar words, see Price's *The Source Book of Play-Party Games*;[1] and for another version of the same, see Wolford, "Down to New Orleans."[2]

"THE GIRL I LEFT BEHIND ME"

1. Oh that girl, that pret-ty lit-tle girl, that girl
I left be-hind me, I'll weep and sigh till the day I
die, for the girl I left be-hind me.

2. Then pass right through and bal-ance too and swing the
girl be-hind you, then turn right back on the same old
track and swing the girl be-hind you.

3. [*Verse three is sung to the tune of the first verse.*]
First gent out to the opposite lady,
Swing her by the right hand.
Swing your partner by the left,
And promenade the girl behind you.

4. [*Verse four is also sung to the tune of the first verse.*]
Oh that girl that pretty little girl,
That girl I left behind me,
Now circle four in a pretty little ring,
And your partner mind you.

5.   [*Verse five is sung to the tune of the second verse.*]
      Quack, quack, quack, goes the pretty little ducks,
      While the old cock's crow gives warning,
      For when the old rooster crows, everybody knows,
      There'll be eggs for breakfast in the morning.

SOURCE: *Mrs. Loren K. Brumley, Dahlgren, Illinois, 1952.*

Formation: Set of four couples in a square.

Action:

Verse 1:   All join hands and circle to the left, during the singing of the first two lines. Each gentleman swings his left hand lady on the third line, and swings his partner on the fourth line.

Verse 2:   Couples one and two face each other, and as they move forward, each passes the opposite by the right shoulder, and then each turns and swings the opposite. After the swinging, number one couple should be on the outside of the set facing the number two couple, with the ladies on the right. Now as they move forward, each passes the opposite by the right shoulder, then each gentleman swings his partner, and each couple returns to their original position.

Verse 3:   The first gentleman swings the opposite lady (the lady of couple three), by the right hand, then both the first and second gentlemen swing their partners by the left hand. The first gentleman promenades with the number two lady and the second gentleman promenades with the number one lady inside the set as couples three and four remain inactive.

Verse 4:   The two couples continue the promenade during the singing of the first two lines. On the third line, the two couples join hands and circle to the left. On the fourth line, gentlemen numbered one and two join both hands with their original partners and swing them around behind them, so that they stand on their right.

Repeat Action:

Verse 2:   Couples one and three repeat verse two above.
Verse 3:   Couples one and three repeat verse three above.
Verse 4:   Couples one and three repeat verse four above.
Verse 2:   Couples one and four repeat verse two above.
Verse 3:   Couples one and four repeat verse three above.
Verse 4:   Couples one and four repeat verse four above.
Verse 1:   All couples do the grand right and left.
Verse 5:   All the gentlemen swing each girl in turn once around.
Verse 1:   All promenade.

The second, third, and fourth couples lead out in turn repeating the actions beginning with the action for verse two.

For similar words to "Girl I Left behind Me," but different tune and actions, see Wolford;[3] Randolph[4] has a similar tune and similar words, but with very meager directions.

"MOLLY BROOKS"

1. Mol--ly Brooks all down in town, all down in
2. Right hand cross all down in town, right hand

town all down in town, Mol-ly Brooks all down in
cross all down in town, right hand back all down in

town and I hope she'll ne-ver re-turn.
town, right hand back all down in town.

3. Break and swing with the op-po-site la-dy, oh I

hope she'll ne-ver re-turn, break and swing with your

own lit-tle la-dy, and I hope she'll ne-ver re-turn.

SOURCE: *Burton Farley, RR 1, Vienna, Illinois, 1946.*

Formation: Set of four couples.

Action:

Verse 1:   All circle left.

Verse 2:   Couple one dances with couple two. The ladies and gentlemen join right hands across and circle to the left during the singing or the first two lines. They join left hands across and circle to the right during the singing of the last two lines.

Verse 3:   Gentlemen swing the opposite ladies during the singing of the first two lines, they swing their partners during the singing of the last two lines.

The first couple moves on to the third couple and the actions for the second and third verses are repeated. Then the first couple moves on to the fourth couple. When the action has been completed with the fourth couple, the couples in the set join hands and circle to the left.

The second couple then leads out and the same actions as done by the first couple are repeated.

For different tune, actions, and words see Wolford [5] and Price; [6] but Randolph [7] has words somewhat the same with different tune and actions.

"FIRST OLD GENT"

Circle eight till you all get straight,
Ladies in the lead and gents follow up.
Halfway round you all went wrong, see-saw back.
Swing your partner and your corner too.
Swing your partner—right and left thru.
Meet your partner and give her a little whirl
All around the outside world. [*Swing all the girls*]
Meet your partner and promenade home.

First old gent out by the right,
Now by the left and don't forget that two arms swing.
Lady round the lady and the gent follow up.
Lady round the gent and gent cuts up.
[*Old gent remains in the center and dances*]

Hook up four in the middle of the floor—Do-si-do.
[*Calls will vary here*]
Swing your opposite to a double "L,"
Swing your honey to a fare-e-well,
Leave that couple and find two more.
[*Repeat lady round etc.—until all couples have danced*]
Home we are—everybody dance. I dance too. [*Men on
inside of circle jig and cut up*]
Meet your partner right hand swing. [*Reverse and jig*]
Meet your partner left hand swing. [*Continues dancing*]
Meet your partner give her a whirl.
Treat them all alike—if it takes all—night.

Swing the complete circle.
Meet your partner and promenade.
Take her out to an easy chair,
Where you take her—
I don't care.

SOURCE: *Kathleen Boswell, Mt. Vernon, Illinois, from Henry Mossenberg,
Mt. Vernon, 1952.*

This figure is sometimes called, "Lady Round the Lady," and is well
known to the older square dancers in the Illinois Ozarks.

6

Singing Games and Chants for Children

Like the play-party games, children's singing games are essentially dramatic, since they involve dialogue, acting, and the assumption of definite roles by the players. They are games only in the sense that all pastimes may be called games. In its stricter sense, a game is the kind of play that involves a contest between players, with winner(s) and loser(s). Games like those listed are often played in this area, especially on the school yard. As far as we can discover, these games never locally suffered the loss of popularity as did the play-party game, which had almost disappeared until revived by new interest several years ago.

FROGGIE'S IN THE MEADOW

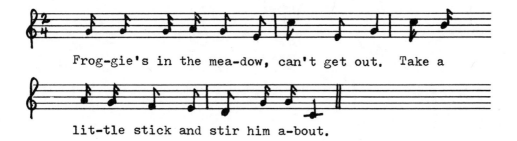

Frog-gie's in the mea-dow, can't get out. Take a

lit-tle stick and stir him a-bout.

2. Froggie's in the meadow, stealing hay.
   Take a little stick and chase him away.

SOURCE: *Clarence J. Buettner, Fults, Illinois, April 5, 1947.*

Formation: Single circle, with one child in the center. Each child has a stick or small switch.

Action: All the children in the circle close their eyes and sing. The boy in the center—the froggie—takes a girl for his partner and runs away and hides. The group sings the song three or more times, until the froggie and his partner are hidden; then all the children hunt for froggie, and the child who finds him becomes the froggie.

The informant, who learned this game from his mother, said the game had the following moral: "You will be punished if you steal."

"HEY LITTLE GIRL"

1. Hey, little girl.   Satisfied!
2. Hey, little girl.   Satisfied!
3. My honey,   Satisfied!
4. Love me.   Satisfied!
5. Come and get me.   Satisfied!
6. Take me 'way.   Satisfied!
7. Hey, Hey!   Satisfied!
8. When I had you.   Hey!
9. You would not do.   Hey!
10. I got somebody.   Hey!
11. And don't want you.   Hey, Hey!

Formation: Single circle with one extra child who stands outside the circle and acts as leader.

Action: During the first seven lines, the circle dances in the counterclockwise direction, using the two-step or step-slide-step, while the leader dances in the opposite direction.

After the fifth line, the leader chooses a partner; after the sixth line, the leader and his partner pretend to walk away. At the end of the seventh line, the dancers in the circle stop in place and tap their feet on the beat and clap their hands off the beat, with two taps and two claps in each measure, while the leader and his partner join right elbows and swing around. After the end of the last line, they swing apart, and a new leader is chosen.

The informant, Mrs. Maggie Branch, described this game as follows: "This is a ring game using a leader, who sings a line, and the players answer. The song is the conversation of a lover and his girl whom he is discarding for another. Only girls played it at our school. When one was chosen, she was the girl. When she was discarded, the first girl went back into the circle, and the second girl became the lover. Thus it went, each one being, first, the loved one, and then, the new lover." For a similar version of this game entitled, "Satisfied," see *Play and Dance Songs and Tunes.*[1]

SOURCE: *Mrs. Maggie Branch, Mounds, Illinois, February 7, 1947.*

"HOW MANY MILES TO BETHLEHEM?"

[*Note: This game is chanted.*]

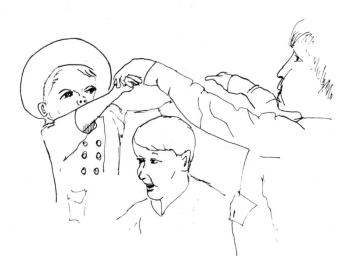

Group: How many miles to Bethlehem?
Reply: Three score miles and ten.
Group: Can we get there by candlelight?
Reply: Yes and back again.
Group: Well here's your bend and here's your bow,
         Open the gates and we will go.

SOURCE: *Mabel Koontz, Xenia, Illinois, January 5, 1952. She said that she learned the game as a school girl in a country school southwest of Flora, Illinois.*

Formation: All the children join hands in a single circle. Two children are chosen to be the gate and also give the reply.

Action: At the end of the chant, the two children, forming the gate, raise their joined hands high to form an arch. (Not both hands, but just the inner right and left hands.)

The two children, standing opposite, lead the circle under the arch. As soon as the leaders pass through the arch, they separate; one child leads his half of the circle to the left, the other leads to the right. When all the children have passed through the arch, the two forming the arch turn under their arms so that all face the same way.

In repeating the game, two other children are chosen to be the gate.

"LITTLE SALLY WALKER"

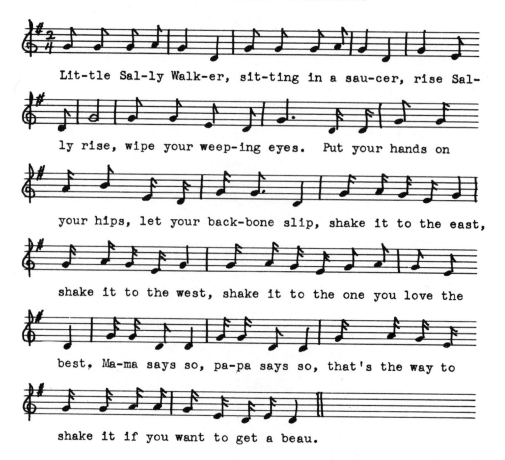

Lit-tle Sal-ly Walk-er, sit-ting in a sau-cer, rise Sal-

ly rise, wipe your weep-ing eyes.   Put your hands on

your hips, let your back-bone slip, shake it to the east,

shake it to the west, shake it to the one you love the

best, Ma-ma says so, pa-pa says so, that's the way to

shake it if you want to get a beau.

SOURCE: *Mrs. Maggie G. Branch, Mounds, Illinois, February 7, 1947.*

Formation: Single circle with one child in the center seated on the floor.

Action: The children in the circle move in a counterclockwise direction, until the word "eyes" is sung.

During the first part of the song, the child in the center pretends to cry. On the words, "rise Sally rise," she gets to her feet and wipes her weeping eyes.

During the remainder of the song, the children in the circle stand in place, while the child in the center does a very agitated dance, shaking her hips to the east, to the west, and to the one she loves the best. Then a shake in honor of mama and papa, and several shakes for good measure.

Another child is chosen and the game is repeated.

For variations of the text, see Wolford [2] and *Play and Dance Songs and Tunes*.[3]

"PAPER OF PINS"

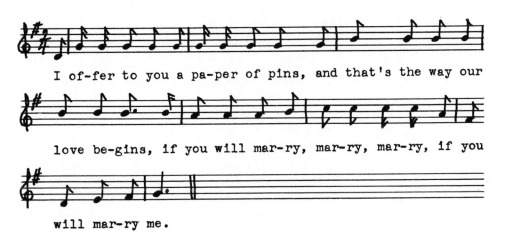

I of-fer to you a pa-per of pins, and that's the way our

love be-gins, if you will mar-ry, mar-ry, mar-ry, if you

will mar-ry me.

Boy: I offer to you a paper of pins,
And that's the way our love begins,
If you will marry, marry, marry,
If you will marry me.

Girl: I'll not accept your paper of pins,
If that's the way our love begins,
And I'll not marry, marry, marry,
And I'll not marry you.

Boy: I offer to you a dress of red,
Stitched all around with golden thread,
If you will marry, marry, marry,
If you will marry me.

Girl: I'll not accept your dress of red,
Stitched all around with golden thread,
And I'll not marry, marry, marry,
And I'll not marry you.

Boy: I offer to you a dress of green,
That you may look just like a queen,
If you will marry, marry, marry,
If you will marry me.

Girl: I'll not accept your dress of green,
That I may look just like a queen,
And I'll not marry, marry, marry,
And I'll not marry you.

Boy: I offer to you a new pair of shoes,
That our true love we may not lose,
If you will marry, marry, marry,
If you will marry me.

Girl: I'll not accept your new pair of shoes,
That our true love we may not lose,
And I'll not marry, marry, marry,
And I'll not marry you.

Boy: I offer to you my hand and heart,
That we may wed and never part,
If you will marry, marry, marry,
If you will marry me.

Girl: I'll not accept your hand and heart,
That we may wed and never part,
And I'll not marry, marry, marry,
And I'll not marry you.

Boy: I offer to you the key to my chest,
That you may have money at your request,

If you will marry, marry, marry,
If you will marry me.

Girl: I will accept the key to your chest,
That I may have money at your request,
And I will marry, marry, marry,
And I will marry you.

Boy: Oh, ho,ho,ho, now isn't that funny,
You don't want me, but you want my money,
And you'll not marry, marry, marry,
And you'll not marry me.

SOURCE: *Delbert A. Waller, Eldorado, Illinois, November 12, 1947.*

Formation: The girls in one line and the boys in the other.

Suggested Action: For a duet with a boy and girl.

As the boy sings, he steps forward and hopefully extends a hand supposedly containing the offer. He has a hopeful expression on his face, which turns to dismay as he retreats step by step, while the girl advances to scorn his offer. Until the boy finishes, the girl keeps her head turned away, then she advances and sings in her scornful way. As the boy offers the key to his money, the girl listens adoringly. But the boy's expression slowly changes to scorn, while she advances with outstretched arms, which he refuses. As she completes her last verse the boy stamps his foot and he begins. "Oh, ho, ho, ho." As he continues, the girl hides her face with her hands and turns away crying.

This game was brought to me by one of my little nine-year-old girls in 1933. She said it was given to her by her grandmother. We once used it at a community meeting, sung by a boy and a girl.

"THE KING'S LAND"

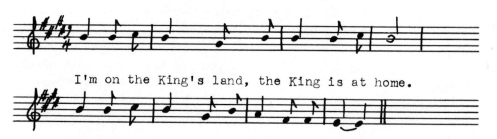

I'm on the King's land, the King is at home.

He can-not catch me un-til I say come.

I'm on the King's land,
The King is at home.
He cannot catch me,
Until I say . . . come.

SOURCE: *Olga Ruether, Grand Chain, Illinois, October 15, 1947.*

Formation: A tree tag game.
Action: Children sing and dance forward upon the forbidden land occupied by the King. The intruders cannot be caught until the last word is sung. The one caught becomes the King.

"PEEP SQUIRREL"

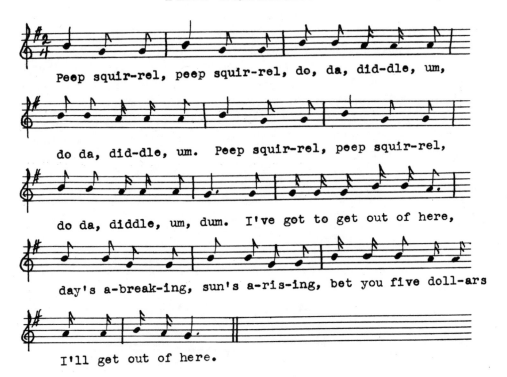

Peep squir-rel, peep squir-rel, do, da, did-dle, um,

do da, did-dle, um. Peep squir-rel, peep squir-rel,

do da, diddle, um, dum. I've got to get out of here,

day's a-break-ing, sun's a-ris-ing, bet you five doll-ars

I'll get out of here.

Group: Peep squirrel, peep squirrel,
            Do, da, diddle, um, do, da, diddle, um.
            Peep squirrel, peep squirrel,
            Do, da, diddle, um.

Squirrel: I've got to get out of here,
            Day's a-breaking,
            Sun's a-rising,
            Bet you five dollars I'll get out
            of here.

SOURCE: *Mr. Charlie Hayes, a former slave, of Klondike, Illinois, by Miss Pattie Cole, Cairo, Illinois, March 26, 1947.*

Formation: Single circle.

Action: As any number may play, all join hands in a tight clasp to form a circle. But the one who represents the "squirrel" stands in the center of the circle. The song is sung, while the "squirrel" goes around the circle trying to break through. When he succeeds in breaking through, he runs for "home." The others try to catch him. If he reaches "home," he is safe. If he is caught before he reaches "home," he is put in the "pen."

The game continues until all have had a chance to be the "squirrel." Those in the pen must pay a penalty, such as, sing a song, do a stunt, tell a story, or anything to add variety.

"YANKEE DOODLE"

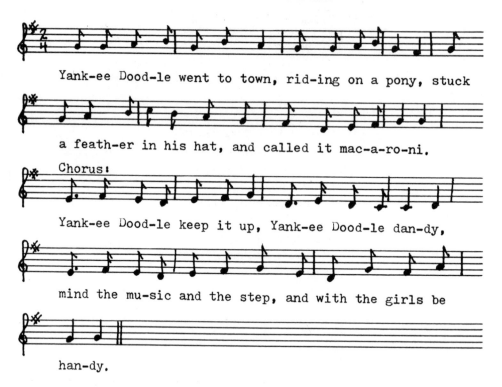

Yank-ee Dood-le went to town, rid-ing on a pony, stuck
a feath-er in his hat, and called it mac-a-ro-ni.
Chorus:
Yank-ee Dood-le keep it up, Yank-ee Dood-le dan-dy,
mind the mu-sic and the step, and with the girls be
han-dy.

SOURCE: *Mrs. Bennie McGowan, Mounds, Illinois, May 8, 1947.*

1. Yankee Doodle went to town,
    Riding on a pony,
    Stuck a feather in his hat,
    And called it macaroni.

First chorus:

    Yankee Doodle keep it up,
    Yankee Doodle dandy,
    Mind the music and the step,
    And with the girls be handy.

2. Let's hoist the window and fall down dead,
    And fall down dead,
    And fall down dead,
    Come Yankee Doodle dandy.

Second chorus:

    Come skipping thru the window,
    And fall down dead, and fall down dead,
    And fall down dead,
    Come Yankee Doodle dandy.

3. Don't miss any window and fall down dead,
    And fall down dead,
    And fall down dead,
    Come Yankee Doodle dandy.

Third chorus:

    Going to knock down sinners,
    And fall down dead, and fall down dead,
    And fall down dead,
    Come Yankee Doodle dandy.

Formation: Single circle with one person, who is to be "Yankee Doodle" in the center.

Action:

Verse 1:   All join hands and circle to the left.

First chorus: All circle to the right.

Verse 2:   All the players in the circle raise their clasped hands to form arches.

Second chorus: The one in the center, "Yankee Doodle," skips in and out through the arches.

Verse 3:   Skipping is continued through the arches.

Third chorus: Players in the circle clasp hands, while the person in the center dances a jig. At the end of this verse, the person in the center chooses another person to be "Yankee Doodle."

"THE NEEDLE'S EYE"

The nee-dle's eye, that does sup-ply the thread that runs

so tru-ly, man-y a beau, have I let go, be-cause I want-

ed you.   Be-cause I want-ed you, be-cause I want-ed you,

man-y a beau have I let go, be-cause I want-ed you.

Oh you look so neat, and you bow so sweet, it al-ways

was my heart's de-sire, to see this cou-ple meet.

SOURCE: *Bernice E. Webster, Centralia, Illinois, November 18, 1948.*

Formation: Players join hands in a single circle. One couple forms a needle's eye by joining left hands in an arch, under which the line may pass.

Action: The circle moves clockwise. The person on the inside of the arch chooses someone from the line by lowering his hands in front of the desired new partner. The chooser quickly joins right hands with his new partner, and swings him around to the inside. The retiring partner moves under the new arch and joins the circle. The new partner is chosen after the last "I wanted you," is sung, as he moves to the outside.

Our informant gave us the following account of her involvement with the game: "I learned the game from Miss Nannie Frank and her sister, Mrs. Myrtle Daggett, who retired from schoolteaching many years ago. They said it was a popular singing game in their group about sixty years ago, in Centralia, Illinois."

For "The Needle's Eye" with a different action and tune, see Wolford,[4] Owens,[5] Price,[6] and Randolph.[7]

"OATS, PEAS, BEANS, AND BARLEY GROW"

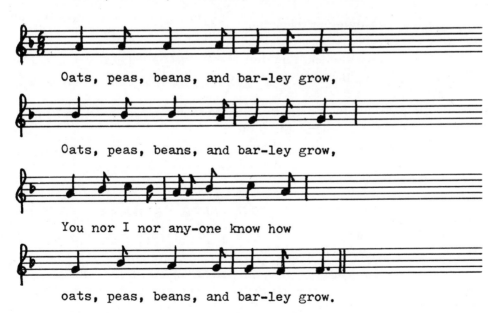

Oats, peas, beans, and bar-ley grow,

Oats, peas, beans, and bar-ley grow,

You nor I nor any-one know how

oats, peas, beans, and bar-ley grow.

SOURCE: *Mrs. Mary Keith, 126 Kirk Street, Anna, Illinois, October 13, 1947.*
Similar versions were obtained from Dorothey V. James, Hurst Bush, Illinois; Pat Neague, Madison, Illinois; and Phyllis Rowland, 303 South State Street, Christopher, Illinois.

1.   Oats, peas, beans, and barley grow,
     Oats, peas, beans, and barley grow,
     You nor I nor anyone know
     How oats, peas, beans, and barley grow.

2.   First the farmer sows the seed,
     Then he stands and takes his ease,
     Stamps his foot, and claps his hands,
     Then turns around to view the land.

3.   Waiting for a partner,
     Waiting for a partner,
     Break the ring and choose one in,
     While all the others dance and sing.

4.   Now you're married, you must obey,
     You must be true to all you say,
     You must be kind, you must be good,
     And help your wife to chop the wood.

Formation: Single circle with one player in the center.

Action: During the singing of the first verse, the players circle to the left.

During the singing of the second verse, all stand in place and follow the action suggested by the words. While singing the first line, the players pretend to sow seeds. Then, they fold their arms and stand at ease while singing the second line. Act out the action suggested while singing the third and fourth lines.

During the singing of the third and last verses, all stand and shake their fingers at the couple in the center.

If the game is repeated, the one chosen is "it."

"OLD GRANNY WIGGINS IS DEAD"

Formation: This game should be played with *fifteen* players or *less*, with *one* player to be the *leader*. All stand in a circle, facing center.

Action: The leader says to the person on his right, "Old Granny Wiggins is dead." The person on the right says, "How did she die?" The leader replies, "Going this way." Then the person on the right repeats what the leader has said as he addresses the person to his right. The dialogue progresses around the entire circle, as the leader adds something to the story each time it progresses.

The first time when the leader says, "Going this way," he extends his right hand shaking it vigorously. The second time, he shakes the left hand.

The third time, he stamps his left foot. The fourth time, he stamps his right foot. The fifth time, he shakes his head.

As each motion is added, the previous motions are continued so that at the fifth time that the dialogue goes round, the players are making all of the motions.

Our informant told us how she remembered learning the game: "My Grandpa Renfro, a white-headed, white-bearded man, taught this game to a group of children at my Grandma Harris's ninetieth birthday party. I was nine years old."

SOURCE: *Mrs. Frances H. Wilhelm, Collinsville, Illinois, July 9, 1949.*

"CLUB FIST"

Action: Several players place their closed hands, one on top of the other, holding to each other's thumbs. The player whose hand is at the bottom of the pile keeps one hand free. When the hands are all in place, the player whose hand is at the bottom says to the player whose hand is on top, "Bag O' Nuts."

The player whose hand is at the bottom says, "Take it off, or knock it off." The player at the top may say, "Take it off," and remove his fist, or he may say, "Knock it off." If he says, "Knock it off," the player whose hand is at the bottom knocks it off with his free hand.

The same procedure is followed with each player until only one fist remains. Then the group asks the following questions which are answered by the person whose fist was on the bottom.

Question:	What have you got in that hole?
Answer:	Bread and cheese.
Question:	Where's my share?
Answer:	The mouse got it.
Question:	Where's the mouse?
Answer:	Cat got it.
Question:	Where's the cat?
Answer:	Fire burnt it.
Question:	Where's the fire?
Answer:	Water quenched it.

Question: Where's the water?
Answer: The ox drank it.
Question: Where's the ox?
Answer: Butcher killed him.
Question: Where's the butcher?
Answer: Dead and buried behind the old church
            door. The first one to crack a smile
            gets one, two, three punches.

SOURCE: *Lucinda Young, 326 North Elm Street, Mounds, Illinois, April 6,
1947.*

The one who gives the answer, then tries to make the other children laugh, grin, or smile so that he can punch them.

7

Rope-Skipping Rhymes

Rope-skipping or rope-jumping rhymes, hand-clapping rhymes, ball-bouncing rhymes, and counting-out rhymes present a varied form of folklore from the standpoint of subject matter and source. The rhymes included here are classified under the following headings:

Rhymes about Parents
Rhymes about Kissing
Nonsense Rhymes
Rhymes about Teachers and Doctors
Rhymes Demanding Special Skills
Double-Rope Rhymes
Rhymes borrowed from Folk Songs, Singing Games, and Mother Goose
Oracles of Divination
Melodrama
Rhymes about Babies
Moral Teaching
Guess Who

In all rope-skipping rhymes, the rope is turned in time with the rhythmic chant so as to hit the ground on each accent of the line.

The rhymes used by children for rope-skipping and other games are a curious combination of sense and nonsense, of wisdom and fun; thus, we have included them in this particular section of our collection.

Rhymes about Parents

Parents offer a fruitful subject for children's rope-jumping rhymes. Here are three that deal in turn with parents as gift givers, as disciplinarians, and as work foremen. For similar versions of number two, see Musick [1] and Nulton.[2]

1. Mama, Mama, don't say a word.
    Papa's going to buy me a mocking bird.
    If the mocking bird don't sing,
    Papa's going to buy me a diamond ring.
    If that diamond ring don't shine,
    Papa's going to buy me a po-ny.
    If that pony runs away,
    Papa's going to buy me a billy goat.
    If that billy goat runs away,
    Papa's going to buy me a dol-ly.
    If that dolly don't say Mama or Papa,
    Papa's going to kick it out the back door.[3]

SOURCE: *Miss Fayne Pearcy, Field School, Mt. Vernon, Illinois, March 1949.*

2. Johnny over the ocean,
    Johnny over the sea,
    Johnny broke a teacup
    And blamed it on me.
    I told Ma,
    Ma told Pa;
    Johnny got a lickin',
    Hee, hee, haw!
    Salt, vinegar,
    Mustard, Pepper! [*Gradual increase of speed*]

SOURCE: *Alice Simons, Kell, Illinois, March 1949.*

3. "Mother, Mother, where's the key?" [*Jump to one end of the rope*]
    "Go ask Father." [*Jump to the other end of the rope*]
    "Have you washed the dishes?" "Yes."
    "Have you swept the floor?" "Yes." [*And so on listing other home chores*]
    "Turn the key in the lock, and run out to play." [*Turn around as you jump, then run out*]

SOURCE: *Carrie Lee Randall, RR 1, Opdyke, Illinois, May 9, 1949.*

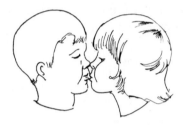

Rhymes about Kissing

Obviously this rhyme is for girls, as it is unlikely that any boys would be involved in a jumping rhyme like this one.

4. Mother, may I go out?
    All the boys are waiting,
    Just to take me out.
    Some will give me candy,
    Some will give me cake.
    Some will give me kisses,
    Behind the garden gate.
    I don't want any candy.
    I don't want any cake.
    But I want [*boy's name*] to kiss me
    Behind the garden gate.

SOURCE: *Miss Fayne Pearcy, Mt. Vernon, Illinois, March 1949.*

Nonsense Rhymes

Several theories have been suggested to explain nonsense words used in rope rhymes and songs. Some may come from other languages and may become distorted, as they are learned orally. Some may be invented to fill out the rhyme, and some are put together just for fun.

5. Aina, mania, mana, mike,
    Bassalona, bona, strike;
    Hare, ware, frown, hock;
    Halico, balico, wee, two ivy whack.

SOURCE: *Doris L. Wood, Omaha, Illinois, April 13, 1949.*

6. Wonery, twoery, tickery seven;
    Alibi, crackaby, ten and eleven;
    Pin, pan, muskyan;
    Tweedle-um, twoddle-um, twenty-won, lerie,
    Ourie, owrie, you are, out! [4]

SOURCE: *Doris L. Wood, Omaha, Illinois, April 13, 1949.*

Rhymes about Teachers and Doctors

This rhyme about teachers surely comes from the past, as the day of
the big stick does not fit in the schools of today.

7. Here comes the teacher with a great big stick,
    Now it's time for arithmetic.
    One and one are two, two and two are four.
    Now it's time for spelling.
    R-a-t spells rat; c-a-t spells cat.
    Now it's time for reading.
    Charlie Chaplin went to France,
    To teach the girlies how to dance.

SOURCE: *Margaret Gillespie, Centerville Station, Illinois, July 9, 1949.*

Number eight expresses a distorted sense of humor. The doctor and
nurse obviously came too late to do anything for the monkey.

8. I had a little monkey,
    His name was Jim.
    I put him in the bathtub,
    To teach him how to swim.
    He drank all the water.
    He ate all the soap.
    He died last night
    With a bubble in his throat.

In came the doctor,
In came the nurse,
In came the little dog with a red purse.
Out went the doctor,
Out went the nurse,
Out went the little dog with a red purse.[5]

SOURCE: *Viola Zachry, Carlyle, Illinois, June 1950.*

9. Mother, Mother I am ill,
Call the doctor from over the hill,
In came the doctor, in came the nurse,
In came the lady with the alligator purse.
I don't want the doctor, I don't want the nurse,
I don't want the lady with the alligator purse.
So out went the doctor, out went the nurse,
Out went the lady with the alligator purse.

SOURCE: *Marie Beiswinger, Fairfield, Illinois, 1949.*

Rhymes Demanding Special Skills

In number ten, after a long rhyming buildup with jumping, the more difficult feats of the split (feet wide apart), high kick, and the kangaroo (feet crossed) are added to test the skill of the jumper.

10. I went up town,
I met Miss Brown,
She gave me a nickel,
I bought a pickle,
The pickle was sour,
I bought some flour.
The flowers were red,
I bought some thread.
The thread was thin,
I bought a pin.
The pin was sharp,
I bought a harp.
And on this harp I played
Spanish Dancer, do the split,

Spanish Dancer, do the split,
Spanish Dancer, do the high kick.
Spanish Dancer, do the Kangaroo,
Spanish Dancer, that will do.

SOURCE: *Helen Reiling, Carmi, Illinois, June 6, 1949.*

11. Donald Duck is a one-legged, one-legged, one-
legged duck. [*Jump on one foot*]
Donald Duck is a two-legged, two-legged, two-
legged duck. [*Jump on both feet*]
Donald Duck is a three-legged, three-legged, three-
legged duck. [*Jump on both feet and one hand*]
Donald Duck is a four-legged, four-legged, four-
legged duck. [*Jump on both feet and hands*]
Donald Duck is a bow-legged, bow-legged, bow-
legged duck. [*Jump bow-legged*]
Donald Duck is a duck! duck! duck!

SOURCE: *Allen Hampton, Marion, Illinois, 1947.*

12. Teddy bear, teddy bear, turn around,
Teddy bear, teddy bear, touch the ground,
Teddy bear, teddy bear, show your shoe,
Teddy bear, teddy bear, that's enough for you. [*Goes out*]
Teddy bear, teddy bear, go back in,
Teddy bear, teddy bear, touch your chin,
Teddy bear, teddy bear, go up stairs,
Teddy bear, teddy bear, say your prayers,
Teddy bear, teddy bear, turn out the light,
Teddy bear, teddy bear, say good night.

SOURCE: *Marie Beiswinger, Fairfield, Illinois, 1949.*

13. Old Man Daisy,
What's makes you so lazy?
Up the ladder, down the ladder. [*Moves toward end*]
One-two-three.
B-B-bumble bee,
Cedar-Cider,
Mustard-Pepper.
One-two-three. [*Hot pepper*]

SOURCE: *Viola Pitt, Breese, Illinois, February 1947.*

14.   Chinaman, Chinaman,
      Walking down the street,
      Chinaman, Chinaman,
      Close your eyes and
      Jump on one foot to nine.

SOURCE: *Viola Pitt, Breese, Illinois, February 1947.*

15.   Around the one that stole the sheep,
      Around the one that ate the meat,
      Around the one that ground the bone,
      Around the one you call your own.
      [*Two jumping—jump around each other*]

SOURCE: *Harriet F. Jordan, Enfield, Illinois, 1949.*

DOUBLE-ROPE RHYMES

These double-rope rhymes demand a great deal of practice and much patience to learn. In number sixteen a long rope is turned by children in the usual manner as the jumper stands in the center of the long rope with an individual rope in her hands which she turns alternately in time with the long rope.

In number seventeen two long ropes are turned alternately, one in each hand of the two children at the ends, one rope is up while the other is down.

16.   Lady, lady, at the gate,
Eating cherries from a plate,
How many cherries did she eat?
1–2–3–4–5 etc.
[*With larger children, use a small rope
inside a big rope, and the child jumping
turns the individual rope.*]

SOURCE: *Carrie Lee Randall, RR 1, Opdyke, Illinois, May 9, 1949.*

17.   Double Dutch, Double Dutch,
Who can jump rope so much?
Faster now, take a bow,
Double Dutch, Double Dutch.

SOURCE: *Ruth Wolfe, Ridgeway, Illinois, October 1950.*

Rhymes Borrowed from Folk Songs, Singing Games, and Mother Goose

The first two lines of number eighteen are taken from the County Antrim folk song "No, John, NO!"

Numbers nineteen, twenty, and twenty-one are adaptations of Mother Goose rhymes. Number twenty-two is an adaptation of a singing game, played like "drop the handkerchief."

18.   On yonder hill there stands a lady,
Who she is, I do not know.
All she wants is gold and silver.
All I want is a bran' new beau.
Go out, [*Name of the one jumping*]
Come in. [*Name of the next in line*]

SOURCE: *Carrie Lee Randall, RR 1, Opdyke, Illinois, May 9, 1949.*

19.   Little Jack Horner,
Sat in a corner [*Squat and eat pie*]

With his pie nearly all eaten up.
And 'twixt finger and thumb
He held a big plum [*Hold up hand*]
And said, "What a good boy am I!" [*The one jumping talks*]

SOURCE: *Carrie Lee Randall, RR 1, Opdyke, Illinois, May 9, 1949.*

20. The autumn is Bo-peep, [*One person*]
The milkweed pods her sheep, [*A named number runs
in and around her, jumping*]
Alas! she cannot find them. [*They run out*]
For where they stood awhile ago,
She finds all hanging in a row,
They've left their tails behind them,

SOURCE: *Carrie Lee Randall, RR 1, Opdyke, Illinois, May 9, 1949.*

21. There was a crooked man,
He walked a crooked mile,
He found a crooked sixpence
Against a crooked stile.
He bought a crooked cat
Which caught a crooked mouse,
And they all lived together in
A little crooked house. [*Jump with feet crossed*]

SOURCE: *Carrie Lee Randall, RR 1, Opdyke, Illinois, May 9, 1949.*

22. [*Child carries a crumpled piece of paper.*]
A tisket, a tasket,
A green and yellow basket,
I lost a letter to my love, [*Drops paper*]
And on the way I found it. [*Stoops to pick up
paper then runs out*]

SOURCE: *Carrie Lee Randall, RR 1, Opdyke, Illinois, May 9, 1949.*

Oracles of Divination

The answers to a large variety of questions are found ranging from weather predictions in number twenty-three, to the number of barrels of beer the "Little Dutchman" can drink in twenty-seven.

23.   All in together, girls,
How is the weather, boys?
Snow! Rain! Sunshine! Sleet!
[*Repeat this line while jumping hot pepper
until a miss on one of the four words.*]
How many days will there be rain?
[*Use the word on which the miss occurred and
jump hot pepper while counting 1–2–3–4 etc.*]
Is it true? [*Jump "yes-no" to hot pepper.*]

SOURCE: *Viola Pitt, Breese, Illinois, February 1947.*

24.   Apples, peaches, creamery butter,
Tell the name of your true lover,
A-B-C-D- [*And so on through the alphabet
until the jumper misses and then a boy is named*]
Billy, Billy, do you love Sally?
Yes, No, Maybe so. Certainly.
[*Repeat until jumper stops on one word which
determines whether he loves her or not.*]
Sally, Sally, do you love Billy?
Yes. No. Maybe so. Certainly.
[*Repeat as before.*]
Sky blue, is it true?
Yes. No. Maybe so. Certainly.
[*Repeat*]

SOURCE: *Margaret Gillespie, Centerville Station, Illinois, July 9, 1949.*

25.   Apples, peaches, creamery butter,
Give me the initials of your lover,
A-B-C-D- [*And so on until the jumper misses*]
What kind of dress are you going to marry in?
What kind of dress are you going to marry in?
Silk, satin, calico, lace [*And so on until jumper misses*]
What kind of house are you going to live in?
What kind of house are you going to live in?
Church, house, barn, pigpen [*And so on until jumper misses*]
How many children are you going to have?
How many children are you going to have?
One, two, three, four, five, six [*And so on until jumper misses*]

SOURCE: *Mrs. Ada L. Fults, Mans, Illinois, January 1948. She said that this
rhyme was played at Canniff School, in Monroe County.*

26. I'm a little Dutch girl all so fat;
    I'm going to get married and what do you think of that?
    I'm not going to marry a butcher, with blood on his toes.
    I'm not going to marry a baker, with flour on his nose.
    I'm not going to marry a king who think's he's everything.
    I'm going to marry a Dutch boy who'll buy me
    a diamond ring.
    How many diamonds will he buy me? [Count]
    What am I going to get married in?
    Silk, satin, calico, rags.
    What am I going to live in?
    House, pigpen or barn.
    How many children will I have? [Count]

SOURCE: *Marie Beiswinger, Fairfield, Illinois, 1949.*

27. I'm a little Dutchman, I drink beer.
    It makes my stomach stick way out here,
    How many barrels can I drink? [Count]

SOURCE: *Marie Beiswinger, Fairfield, Illinois, 1949.*

28. I went down to my grandpa's farm,
    I chased that billy goat around the barn,
    I love coffee, I love tea,
    How many kicks did he give to me? [Count]
    [Child jumps until he misses]

SOURCE: *Doris L. Wood, Omaha, Illinois, April 13, 1949.*

Melodrama

29. Last night and the night before,
        Twenty-four robbers knocked at the door.
    I went upstairs to get my gun,
        And by mistake, I shot my son.
    I went downstairs to get my knife,
        And by mistake, I stabbed my wife.
    I ran upstairs to wash my dishes,
        And by mistake, I washed my britches.

SOURCE: *Mr. James Jordan, Carmi, Illinois, May 1949.*

Rhymes about Babies

This seems an indelicate way to treat a baby, but children are not always inclined to be delicate.

30. Fudge, fudge, tell the judge
    Mama has a newborn baby.
    Wrap it up in tissue paper,
    Send it down the elevator.
    First floor, second floor . . . eighth floor,
    And out the back door.

SOURCE: *Miss Fayne Pearcy, Mt. Vernon, Illinois, March 1949.*

Moral Teaching

A simple counting-out rhyme is here augmented to include the ultimate punishment for wrongdoing. A shorter version of number thirty-one is found in Musick.[6]

31. One-two-three-four-five-six-seven
    All good children go to Heaven.
    When they get there, God will say,
    "Where's that diamond, you stole that day?"
    If you say you do not know,
    He will send you down below,
    Where it's H-O-T. [*Hot pepper*] [7]

SOURCE: *Mrs. Mary Dagley, Crossville, Illinois, February 1949.*

Guess Who

Young girls are not reluctant to give a clue of affection to the boy they like, as this rhyme indicates.

32. Strawberry shortcake, gooseberry pie.
    Tell the initials of your honeypie.
    [*Say A, B, C, etc. Run out on the
    friend's initials.*]

SOURCE: *Helen Reiling, Carmi, Illinois, June 6, 1949.*

References, Notes & Index

REFERENCES

Ames, L. D., Mrs. "The Missouri Play-Party." *Journal of American Folklore* 24 (1888): 295–318.

Arnold, Byron. *Folksongs of Alabama.* University: University of Alabama Press, 1950.

Bartlett, John Russell. *Dictionary of Americanisms.* New York: Boston, Little, Brown, 1859.

Belden, Henry M. *Ballads and Songs Collected by the Missouri Folk-lore Society.* Columbia: University of Missouri, 1940.

Chase, Richard. *Old Songs and Singing Games.* Chapel Hill: University of North Carolina Press, 1938.

Child, Francis James. *English and Scottish Popular Ballads.* New York: Folk Lore Press, 1957.

Drake, Robert Y., Jr. "Casey Jones: The Man and the Song." *Tennessee Folklore Society Bulletin* 19, no. 4 (December 1953): 95–101.

Leach, MacEdward. *The Ballad Book.* New York: Harper, 1955.

Morris, Alton C. *Folksongs of Florida.* Gainesville: University of Florida Press, 1950.

Musick, Ruth Ann, and Vance Randolph. "Children's Rhymes from Missouri." *Journal of American Folklore* 63 (1950): 430.

Neely, Charles. *Tales and Songs of Southern Illinois.* Edited by John W. Spargo. Menasha, Wisconsin: George Banta Publishing, 1938.

Nulton, Lucy. "Jump Rope Rhymes as Folk Literature." *Journal of American Folklore* 61 (1948): 54.

Owens, William A. *Swing and Turn: Texas Play-Party Games.* Dallas: Tardy Publishing, 1936.

Play and Dance Songs and Tunes. Archive of Folk Song. Library of Congress, AFF-L9.

Pound, Louise. "Traditional Ballads in Nebraska." *Journal of American Folklore.* Reprint 1913.

Price, M. Katherine. *The Source Book of Play-Party Games.* Minneapolis: Burgess Publishing, 1949.

Randolph, Vance. *Ozark Folksongs*. Vol. 3. Columbia: State Historical Society of Missouri, 1946.

————. *Who Blowed Up the Church House?* New York: Columbia University Press, 1952.

Sandburg, Carl. *The American Songbag*. New York: Harcourt, Brace, 1927.

Scarborough, Dorothy. *A Song Catcher in the Southern Mountains*. New York: Columbia University Press, 1937.

Seeger, Ruth Crawford. *American Folk Songs for Christmas*. Garden City, N. Y.: Doubleday, 1953.

Sharp, Cecil J. *English Folk Songs from the Southern Appalachians*. 2d ed., enl. Vol. 2. London: Oxford University Press, 1932.

Smith, Reed. *South Carolina Ballads*. Cambridge, Mass: Harvard University Press, 1928.

Standard Dictionary of Folklore. 2 vols. Edited by Maria Leach. New York: Funk & Wagnalls, 1950.

Thomas, Jean, and Joseph A. Leeder. *Singin' Gatherin'*. New York: Silver, Burdett, 1939.

Wolford, Leah Jackson. *The Play-Party in Indiana*. Indianapolis: Indiana Historical Commission, 1916.

NOTES

1. Songs of Local Significance

1 Neely, p. 26.
2 *Saint Genevieve Herald*, August 17, 1935.
3 Lena Moore, 407 East Church, Benton, Illinois, April 24, 1951.
4 *Shawnee News*, August 13, 1896.
5 Ibid., April 14, 1898.
6 Drake, pp. 95–109.
7 Sharp, p. 7.

2. Traditional Folk Songs

1 *Standard Dictionary of Folklore*, 2:1033.
2 Child, p. 95.
3 Mrs. Lessie Parrish, Carbondale, Illinois, November 12, 1937.
4 Smith, pp. 80–94.
5 Leach, p. 9.
6 Randolph, *Ozark Folksongs*, pp. 171–74.
7 Randolph, *Who Blowed Up the Church House?* pp. 153–55.
8 Belden, pp. 237–39.
9 Morris, pp. 368–70.
10 Owens, pp. 175–76.
11 Wolford, pp. 93–94.
12 Neely, pp. 175–76.
13 *Standard Dictionary of Folklore*, 2:635.
14 Neely, pp. 172–75.
15 Arnold, pp. 72–73.
16 Morris, pp. 356–58.
17 Randolph, *Ozark Folksongs*, pp. 280–82.
18 Scarborough, pp. 336–45.
19 Arnold, p. 68.
20 Belden, pp. 66–67.
21 Morris, pp. 295–300.
22 Owens, pp. 46–47.
23 Randolph, *Ozark Folksongs*, pp. 143–48.
24 Sandburg, p. 385.
25 Leach, pp. 297–98.
26 Child, p. 95.
27 Sharp, pp. 6–9.
28 Belden, p. 225.
29 Owens, pp. 228–29.
30 Randolph, *Ozark Folksongs*, pp. 318–23.
31 Leach, pp. 747–48.
32 Pound, pp. 364–66.
33 Belden, pp. 148–50.
34 Morris, pp. 346–49.
35 Owens, pp. 91–92.
36 Randolph, *Ozark Folksongs*, pp. 258–61.
37 Sandburg, pp. 68–69.
38 Scarborough, pp. 260–64.
39 Bartlett, p. 1238.
40 *Standard Dictionary of Folklore*, 1:427.

41 Arnold, pp. 12–13.
42 Belden, pp. 494–99.
43 Morris, pp. 407–15.
44 Owens, pp. 254–56.
45 Randolph, *Ozark Folksongs*, pp. 402–10.
46 Sandburg, p. 143.
47 Scarborough, pp. 244–46.

3. Singing Games: Contra Formation

1 Randolph, *Ozark Folksongs*, pp. 362–64.
2 Thomas and Leeder, pp. 18–19.
3 Chase, pp. 45.
4 Owens, pp. 13.
5 Price, pp. 43.
6 Randolph, *Ozark Folksongs*, pp. 297–301.

4. Singing Games: Single Circle Formation

1 Wolford, pp. 80–81.
2 Ibid., p. 36.
3 Ibid., p. 96.
4 Owens.
5 Price, p. 115.
6 Randolph, *Ozark Folksongs*, pp. 313–14.
7 Ames, pp. 295–318.
8 Wolford, p. 97.
9 Webb J. Kimmel, RFD, Thompsonville, Illinois, November 10, 1948.
10 James M. Jordan, 105 Herbert Ave., Carmi, Illinois, March 2, 1949.
11 Mrs. Thad Boston, 1106 South Hickory St., Centralia, Illinois, December 2, 1948.
12 Annie M. Trainer, 108 Wabash, Belleville, Illinois, October 28, 1953.
13 Yvonne Briley, Thompsonville, Illinois, July 20, 1954.

14 William Lockard, Makanda, Illinois, November 16, 1947.
15 Bessie Gayer, West Frankfort, Illinois, obtained this version from Bonnie Homan, 304 Orchard St., Ziegler, Illinois, January 19, 1954.
16 Velma Reynolds, Waltonville, Illinois, March 28, 1948.
17 B. R. Gholson, Broughton, Illinois, March 17, 1953.

5. Singing Squares

1 Price, p. 43.
2 Wolford, p. 41.
3 Ibid., p. 46.
4 Randolph, *Ozark Folksongs*, pp. 352–54.
5 Wolford, p. 71.
6 Price, p. 75.
7 Randolph, *Ozark Folksongs*, p. 75.

6. Singing Games and Chants for Children

1 *Play and Dance Songs and Tunes*, AFF-L9.
2 Wolford, p. 86.
3 *Play and Dance Songs and Tunes*, AFF-L9.
4 Wolford, p. 72.
5 Owens, p. 9.
6 Price, p. 161.
7 Randolph, *Ozark Folksongs*, pp. 351–52.

7. Rope-Skipping Rhymes

1 Musick and Randolph, p. 430.
2 Nulton, p. 60.
3 Ibid., pp. 54.
4 Musick and Randolph, p. 428.
5 Nulton, p. 58.
6 Musick and Randolph, p. 431.
7 Ibid., p. 431.

INDEX